MW00487846

'Katherine Doggrell analyses the struggles for market between hotels, the sharing economy and the online travel agents in a lively way. For us business folk who just use the beds but work in the many industries about to be disrupted by the impact of AI, FinTech, climate change or variants of the sharing economy the lessons are numerous.'

Mark Moody-Stuart, former chairman of Royal Dutch Shell and Anglo American Plc, author of Responsible Leadership

'An excellent analysis of why Airbnb and the sharing economy has made such inroads into the traditional hotel market. Katherine Doggrell delivers a punchy wake-up call to the chains who treat guests as a mere commodity.'

Ruth Watson, hotelier, broadcaster and food writer

'In the style of Brad Stone's *The Everything Store, Checking Out* provides readers with a well-researched and insightful deep-dive into the development of the sharing economy and in particular how it affects the hospitality sector. Katherine's investigative style helps highlight issues and perspectives hitherto less visible, making this an essential read for anyone wanting to truly understand the future of the hotel sector.'

Peter O'Connor, Professor at ESSEC Business School and author of Reviewed

'I really enjoyed reading this book, Katherine's writing style is wonderful, particularly the way she brings humour into an insightful journey through the rise of the sharing economy and its impact on the hotel industry. Anyone who can bring references to Prince and cricket whilst being informative at the same time gets my vote!'

Will Hawkley, Global Head of Leisure & Hospitality, KPMG

'*Checking Out* expertly analyses the threat of the sharing economy, and what the traditional hospitality sector can do to survive. I have always enjoyed Katherine's writing style, and she is one of the leading commentators on the hospitality and leisure sector. This book is a must-read for those linked to the industry who wish to remain ahead of the game – or for those that simply appreciate a good book!'

Tim Helliwell, Head of Hotels, Barclays Bank

Checking Out

What the rise of the sharing economy means for the future of the hotel industry

Katherine Doggrell

BLOOMSBURY BUSINESS

LONDON • OXFORD • NEW YORK • NEW DELHI • SYDNEY

BLOOMSBURY BUSINESS
Bloomsbury Publishing Plc
50 Bedford Square, London, WC1B 3DP, UK

BLOOMSBURY, BLOOMSBURY BUSINESS and the Diana logo are
trademarks of Bloomsbury Publishing Plc

First published in Great Britain 2020

A catalogue record for this book is available from the British Library

Library of Congress Cataloguing-in-Publication data has been applied for

ISBN: HB: 978-1-4729-6872-2; eBook: 978-1-4729-6871-5

2 4 6 8 10 9 7 5 3 1

Typeset by Deanta Global Publishing Services, Chennai, India
Printed and bound in Great Britain by CPI Group (UK) Ltd, Croydon CR0 4YY

To find out more about our authors and books visit www.bloomsbury.com
and sign up for our newsletters

For Cameron and Philip, my loves
And for the hotel sector, which puts a roof over my head

CONTENTS

Introduction

I love hoteliers. If you want to stay up until dawn with the friendliest, smartest, 'most-likely to have been arrested in Ghana for looking at a statue without a permit' people, find yourself a bottle and a hotelier and pull up a wingback chair. But hotels and I are on rocky ground.

The schism first dawned the morning after the night before, as schisms are often wont to do. Waking up with no clear idea of where you are is not limited to excess, but a feature of the global hotel market. The classic design of bed-with-en suite has barely changed since Mary and Joseph decided they'd rather not share with the donkey after all, and one blearily viewed room looks almost exactly like another, no matter what the neon sign over the door.

The world is on the move, in its billions, but while there is more to distract us, there is also more to isolate us. More people live and work alone and have less human contact. Spending the evening in another anonymous box does not warm the soul. As we travel more, we value the comforts of home and that which revives us.

This millennium has seen a shift away from hotel ownership and into franchising for the big hotel chains, as well as a shift in how the operators view the consumer. Where the head in the bed used to be the customer, as the source of their fees and the degrees of separation from the brand and the guest have grown, so the real estate investor has become the more relevant customer for the branded companies.

The global hotel companies live and die by their pipeline: the volume of rooms they are gushing across the planet every quarter. Many a CEO has been jettisoned after failing to maintain a suitable flow and the structure of the sector has shifted to feed this passion for limitless growth. The need to lure hotel investors with fresher, more delicious brands has led to a proliferation of flags. Already got one hotel in London? Never mind, we've got a whole new brand coming, why not have one of those as well? Why not collect the whole set?

While owners were being told that brands were all different – the better to avoid territorial arguments – to the head in the bed, they all looked very similar. Bed factories, in other words, with only return on investment (ROI) in mind. Branding has made everywhere familiar and nowhere memorable and, in the rush to expand around the world, the art of hospitality has been lost.

Enter the sharing economy. Invisible to the naked eye, it blended perfectly into the neighbourhood (until after dark, when – for the unlucky few – the sound of hen nights filled the air). The camouflaged threat, the Predator that the hotel sector wakes up sweating about … untold numbers of rooms, apartments, houses, yurts, treehouses, yachts, islands. And the degree of separation from the owner was often only one wall.

Airbnb, which dominated the sector and has become the noun-to-verb Hoover of letting people sleep in your spare room, had 7 million listings by 2019, making market leader Marriott International, with 1.4 million rooms[1], look like a weekend driver. But it was what was included in those listings that was chilling the 3am sweat on the foreheads of those in the hotel sector. The company was a moving target, vehemently protecting where its hosts were, with hotels aware that, even if locations were revealed, they were not always on the market, coming up for rent as and when the *owners*, not Airbnb, decided. Were they just rooms? Or whole castles? Were they fold-out beds in apartments reeking of patchouli? Or were they Instagram-worthy penthouses over Manhattan? Transparency

---

[1]Marriott International, 5 November 2018

is not the watchword of homesharers and the nature of the offer is that it was in constant flux.

The hospitality sector has been unable to agree on the impact of homesharing on its business. In 2014, Richard Solomons, the then-CEO of InterContinental Hotels Group (IHG), said on the sidelines at Davos that homesharing wasn't a threat because IHG was focused on the business guest instead[2]. By 2017, Accor chairman and CEO Sébastien Bazin was saying: 'Airbnb took from us, we will take from them'[3].

Airbnb said it had seen more than 400 million guest arrivals since 2008 and those could all be travellers who wouldn't have packed a bag had homesharing not been an option. It must also include jaded old road warriors desperate to once, maybe just once, slump back on a sofa and eat some soup rather than sit cross-legged on a bed with their laptop, waiting an hour for a tepid club sandwich to arrive from room service. Parents who wanted bedrooms on the same floor as their children. Friends who wanted their own social space. Today's consumer wanted *experience*, a story to tell when they got back home.

The hotel sector was not alone in facing disruption from an online platform. That the challenge came when the rise of the online travel agents (OTAs) reduced rooms to a mere commodity – traded by cost, not the actual experience – only served to heighten the issue.

The sharing economy was never just about rooms; it was about redefining what hospitality is, what true service meant and realising that it was no longer wearing a white jacket with gilt buttons. Homesharing came with the promise that you could feel at home while being away, that you could be part of a community and learn about more than you could when staying in a room that looks exactly the same in Albuquerque, Bangkok or

---

[2]www.wsj.com/articles/ihg-ceo-airbnb-homesharing-sites-should-be-regulated-1390472221
[3]www.afr.com/real-estate/commercial/hotels-and-leisure/airbnb-took-from-us-we-will-take-from-them-accor-ceo-20170504-gvynfd

Cardiff. That you would be greeted with warmth, not the demand for your credit card in case you went on a thieving spree. That you could put some beers in the fridge and then drink them. In the light. And not the light of the bathroom while you sit on the toilet.

The sharing economy is now being attacked from within, facing the challenge of growing numbers of professional investors who will affect how well it keeps its homespun image, but for the time being the challenge lies with the hotels. There was a time when the hotel sector introduced the world to the wonder of electricity, the marvel of room service, the novelty of the ice machine. Does it once again have the power to inspire love and loyalty? Or will it be marginalised as a relic from a bygone age?

Unless otherwise attributed, all quotes are the product of an interview with the author. It is time to give the hotel sector its say, in its own words.

PART ONE

THERE'S SOMEBODY AT THE DOOR – WHAT IS AIRBNB AND HOMESHARING?

The story of how Airbnb's founders skimmed off the bubbling overflow of San Francisco's conference market and charged it to sleep on their sofa is one destined to go down in start-up lore as a damn-so-obvious moment.

Since 2008, Brian Chesky, Joseph Gebbia Jr. and Nathan Blecharczyk have overseen Airbnb's growth from sofa surfing to platform to asset class. Along the way, it has become the vacuum cleaner of the sharing economy; you Airbnb on holiday, and Airbnb your flat to pay for it. Other brands are out there getting couches on to the market – HomeAway, Onefinestay, Vrbo – but only Airbnb has graduated to verb status.

As with many of the online players that live as apps but not on the high street, what Airbnb represented was largely in the eye of the beholder; as a competitor, the hotel industry found not being able to nail down where Airbnb was, what its rates were and who was using it on any given night to be incredibly frustrating. In the wider economy, what Airbnb and those

who would ape it meant to your customers, your business and your tax
payers swung across the spectrum from help to hindrance, and such a
vivid spectrum and differing assessment of what homesharing actually is
has led to a rainbow of different responses. The closer Airbnb came into
the light cast by its looming initial public offering (IPO) the closer it came
to transparency and yet, as with those other technology businesses for
which bricks and mortar was no restraint, it could quickly and nimbly
evolve like so much Lego – and be just as painful for those who found
it underfoot.

Airbnb's mission, it said, was 'to create a world where people
can belong through healthy travel that is local, authentic, diverse,
inclusive and sustainable. Airbnb uniquely leverages technology to
economically empower millions of people around the world to unlock
and monetise their spaces, passions and talents to become hospitality
entrepreneurs'.[1]

By 2019, the platform laid claim to more than 7 million[2] listings, with
an average of over 2 million people staying in an Airbnb per night. Its
next-largest rival, HomeAway, had 1.8 million[3] listings. Listings could
be duplicated across platforms, feature whole or partial properties, and
not always be available, depending on the solvency requirements of the
host. They might be country houses, teepees or treehouses. The flexibility
and opaque nature of the sharing platforms meant that the real footprint
of these beasts could only be seen in the impression they left on the
performance and activity of their rivals, and in the locations where they
appeared, even only briefly.

The hotel sector, which could be identified more easily – by the
illuminated 'hotel' sign over the door – had, according to STR Global[4],

---

[1] Airbnb, November 2018
[2] https://news.airbnb.com/update-on-the-airbnb-community/
[3] Expedia Group results, Q3 2018
[4] STR February 2018

16.9 million revenue-generating properties of 10 rooms or more available for public consumption around the world in 2018. Registration, inspection and taxation regimes meant that once the sign was hoisted, change of use was not undertaken on a nightly basis, unlike the fluid state of peer-to-peer lodging.

Tracking homesharing, then, was a matter not only of volume, but also of influence. As one grew, so did the other.

In plain sight – hospitality's hall of mirrors

For the hotel sector, a refusal to look directly at homesharing and acknowledge it was the story of how Airbnb managed to make inroads into a segment not known for its rapid embracing of innovation. More on 'the Internet and how it won't catch on' later in this book. What Airbnb was, and what it meant for the travel sector, ran the gamut from distribution platform to a whole new form of hospitality depending on who was looking. And behind it all, the new contender itself had no incentive to reveal exactly where it was and how it was operating, which really didn't feel like playing fair.

In 2014, Richard Solomons, then-CEO, InterContinental Hotels Group[5], told a meeting at the World Economic Forum (WEF) in Davos that Airbnb did not compete with IHG, since around 60 per cent of IHG's volume was business travel[6]. Airbnb launched its Airbnb for Business segment in 2014, shortly after Solomons' comments, proving that Davos was worth the ticket price for Airbnb, packing a strategic punch that proved that the WEF wasn't all Blofeld stroking his cat in a mountain

---

[5] 864,699 hotel rooms globally as at 10 November 2019, the company that brings you Holiday Inn, InterContinental and 13 other flags. The group most likely to be described as a bid target by all observers, but that – at the time of writing – had somehow slipped the noose.
[6] *Wall Street Journal*, 23 January 2014

lair. By 2018, the division had been renamed Airbnb for Work and soon
accounted for 15 per cent of bookings. Miaow.

By 2019, Sébastien Bazin, chairman and CEO at Accor[7], described
Airbnb as 'wake-up call'. He added: 'Clients have evolved, they are more
picky, they want something more local, cheaper, unique, more experience
driven. [Airbnb] is showing that those youngsters are sick and tired of
anything which is standardised, which has rooms that look like each
other whether you are in São Paulo or Melbourne. We had to go from
being product-minded for 50 years to being client-minded, which is a
major shift.'

As to the form of this threat, homesharing was, says James Bland,
director at BVA BDRC, 'a multifaceted thing'. He said: 'It was like email
was to the letter. We always communicated, we always sent each other
messages of communication, it was just that we had to do it over the space
of a couple of weeks and it was a bit of a pain and they were expensive
to send. [Now] we can send lots and lots of stuff all the time and do it
relatively cheaply in terms of the fulfilment and transactions costs, and in
many respects Airbnb is that. It is a platform, but it is extending something
which existed already, to this global animal of a business. To some it's a
community, to some it's just a cheap accommodation site, to some it's a
way of life, to others it's an income source.'

Hiding in plain sight was also the view of Marieke Dessauvagie, hotel
consultant at Colliers International, who believed homesharing was far
from unique. Instead, it was something that had been done for years, with
Airbnb merely making it easier for hosts to rent their apartments and for
guests to find them, thus spawning a new group of potential hoteliers. She
said: 'You are in every sense of the word a host; you welcome your guests,

---

[7]704,000 hotel rooms globally as at 4 March 2019, the company that brings you Ibis, Raffles and
28 other flags. Beloved by sector hacks as Bazin is seemingly incapable of making it through a
week without buying one or more companies and confusing the heck out of the other CEOs in
the process.

you make sure your house is tidy, you might spend some time with them. Everyone who is a host on Airbnb is part of the hospitality industry.'

Hospitality attracted the hospitable – it attracted Dessauvagie herself to list on Airbnb in her home town of Amsterdam, until the city's rules were tightened – and it attracted those for whom a stay away from home should always be more than somewhere to lay your head and perhaps eat a budget-breaking macadamia nut from the minibar at 11pm. Imran Hussain, director at collaborative marketing communications agency THC/Endeavour and one of those for whom passion for the sector ranked even higher than the thread count at The Savoy, took a look at Airbnb and called it as: 'Cheap. Travel. Tourism. Freedom. Choice. And, as Neo said best in *The Matrix*, the problem is choice.'

Robin Sheppard, chairman at Bespoke Hotels[8], and a colleague of Hussain, described homesharing as 'a generational revolution which is already deeply embedded, with individuals letting apartments in an organised, maximum bandwidth fashion'.

There were those for whom describing homesharing as anything on the scale of revolution was akin to describing the belt buckle worn by Hans Christian Andersen's naked emperor as a step forwards in clothes fastenings. James Chappell, global business director at Horwath HTL, was sceptical of seeing Airbnb as anything other than a decent bit of technology, a good piece of marketing and a very good website, which, he pointed out, wasn't something that you could accuse hotels of being. This – along with the rise of the OTAs – was more than enough to spook the sector and certainly more than enough for it to have an impact. The rise in prominence of the sharing platform as the bogeyman of choice at industry events was also, he pointed out, down to the 'absence of anything

---

[8]225 hotels as at June 2018, the company was one of the largest privately owned hotel groups in the UK. Co-founder Sheppard was one of the hoteliers' hoteliers, the author of a book on his encounter with Guillain-Barre syndrome and who revolutionised the performance of a pub in Bath by launching a philosophy night on unsuspecting locals. Underachievers look away now.

else to talk about'. When Chip Conley, founder of Joie de Vivre Hospitality, joined Airbnb[9], 'people thought that, if there's a hotel guy there now, it must have something to do with hotels'. And you cannot fault that logic in a sector where people are born, raised and die hotels.

For James Woudhuysen, a visiting professor at London South Bank University and also a futurologist, Airbnb was: 'a low-cost, convenient, ink-jet printer. Do I think it's an exemplar of how the world is moving in every sector towards a sharing economy? Absolutely not. I don't buy the sharing economy, I don't buy the management speak about disruption. Airbnb, like Uber, is useful and convenient, but it's not that innovative. If you're satisfied with that and that's the way that society is going to evolve, then I'm not on that bus. It's just not strong enough, it's just not interesting enough, it's just not employment-generating enough. With Airbnb, it's about sweating the asset, but that's no way forward for society. There's no investment, you're not taking a risk, you don't innovate, you don't change the experience much, only a bit.

'Airbnb is part of a number of developments out of Silicon Valley which are to do with IT platforms, and I believe those to be useful and convenient and have their place, but they're not the radical innovation that is often praised to the heavens. IT is regarded as a panacea and a reasonable interface is regarded as amazing and worthy of a market capitalisation – in Uber's case of about $70 billion – so Airbnb, it's a complete bubble.'

Woudhuysen made a point. The sector needed to consider whether Airbnb met the criteria laid out in Clayton Christensen's *The Innovator's Dilemma* – where successful companies could do everything right, but were disrupted to the extent that they lost out to new, unexpected competitors who can rise and take over the market. For that, the impact on performance had to be assessed and for that, the view of the investors had to be gauged.

---

[9]In 2013. He scaled back to 'advisor' in 2017, but the damage was already done in the eyes of frightened hoteliers.

Follow the money: was Airbnb eating my cheese?

In the 2000s, the hotel sector had embraced selling off the family jewels with a vigour not seen since Jack was instructed to take the cow to the market and not to come back without something for the pot. The magic beans took root and while your parents might not have realised that the local Hilton[10] wasn't actually owned by Hilton, that didn't matter, because there were now so many more Hiltons that Paris, Nicky and all the other Hiltons didn't have to own them[11]. Hilton had become more than a local hotel; it had become a brand. And brands didn't need bricks to hold them up.

Hotels became big business. In 2017, Hilton – now publicly owned, sorry Paris – reported revenues of $9.14 billion; Marriott International, the largest branded operator in the sector, had revenues of $22.89 billion in the same year. €1.93 billion for Accor. $1.78 billion for IHG. There was much here to attract investors and much for them to start feeling possessive about if they started to lose out to the sofa across the street.

The hotel operators had, Accor aside, yet to admit to the pinch of the peer-to-peer lodging sector. When asked about the impact of Airbnb in May 2017, Arne Sorenson, president and CEO at Marriott International[12], told analysts that the impact of sharing platforms had been 'less impactful

---

[10]954,855 rooms at September 2019, which brings you the Hilton and Waldorf Astoria brands, plus 12 others. The company steadfastly refuses to buy other companies' brands, but the sector allows it because when they launch their own brands – as it did with Denizen in 2009 – it can lead to lawsuits that keep us all entranced for months.

[11]When asked why he opened a second Krabby Patty next to the first in *Spongebob Squarepants the Movie*, Mr Krabs said: 'For the money' and it's much the same for Hilton.

[12]1.4 million rooms, the sector's behemoth following its takeover of Starwood Hotels & Resorts. The company that brings you Courtyard and Ritz Carlton, with 28 other brands in between. Stay in a Marriott room and you will find both the Gideon Bible and the Book of Mormon. The group has a history of being close to politics – former presidential candidate Mitt Romney was a board member – but this blew itself out with the arrival in power of that other hotelier, Donald Trump.

to the RevPAR [revenue per available room] numbers that we've posted the last number of years than folks might have imagined. They are serving a different customer than what we serve at Marriott. They are skewed much more towards leisure. They are skewed much more towards a value-centric customer in the bulk of their business. I'm not necessarily sure that this customer immediately pops up and shows up in our hotel suites.'

And this had better remain the case when it came to hotels, because those who owned the properties upon which the operators hoisted their logos would be peeved if things changed. Other asset classes were, after all, available to real estate investors. David Harper, head of valuations at Hotel Partners Africa and author of *Valuation of Hotels for Investors*[13] warned that: 'Airbnb can clearly impact on hotel values, just by taking potential bookings away from a hotel – that loss of business impacts the revenue and profit generated, in turn lowering the value of the property, as property values are based on the trading potential. Indeed, as Airbnb becomes more popular, the proportion of local demand directed at this segment will mean hotels will need to either replace this "lost business" with other segments of business, or they will see values drop. Airbnb has different penetration rates in different market segments – it is much more popular with the FIT [free independent travellers] travelling for leisure than it is with business travellers or with group travellers. As such, hotels and resorts catering to this demographic are more at risk from losing business – and value – than business or conference-based operations.'

So, thinking back to Solomons at Davos, hotels continued to bet on business.

---

[13]And *Hotels & Resorts, an Investor's Guide*. Also chairman of the MCC (Madness Cricket Club), which arranges games of cricket to raise money for Cancer Research, including one up Kilimanjaro, which got David and the rest of the team, many of whom pop up in these pages, into the *Guinness Book of Records* for the highest-ever game of cricket. Sure he can value hotels, but his life?

The belief that the homesharing sector was one driven by consumers looking for cheap stays, rather than a different type of stay – witness Airbnb's promise of 'Don't go there, live there' – was a reassuring bead on the sector's string of worries. Anything happening at the lower end of the market, which didn't have an impact on the lucrative corporate customer, could be seen as an aberration. Dessauvagie said: 'The main driver is pricing. It is often said that the price is the same as a hotel room and in some cities it is, but in the end the price per person per night is cheaper. The second driver has to do with experience, of being in the home of a local, but I think that comes second to price.'

Hussain was willing to blame price for the use of peer-to-peer lodging, but also lay some of the fault at the door of the hotels themselves, which may have taken the idea of 'captive market' just that bit too literally and pushed consumers into cheaper options by having become a little giddy with pricing. He commented: 'If it weren't for price, if you neutralised hotel rates across the world, would Airbnb have arrived? Airbnb is here because hoteliers have failed to correctly communicate their pricing policy. You want to drive the rates so you can up your asset valuation, so you can make another hotel, so you can bank it, and that's true for brands and independents. You start to wonder, if it weren't for Airbnb, would the same hotel pricing continue? There is some degree of "Oh my God, London's full, jack your rates up" and that mentality can't survive, it's unfair. Hotels will have to think of new ways.'

Not afraid to slap a number on motivation by price was Morgan Stanley, which, in November 2018, released the results of a survey reporting that 55 per cent of those who either used or planned to use Airbnb said that price was one of the three most important factors that led them to use or plan to use the service, in line with the previous year. This was 1.6 times larger than 'location' and 2.1 times larger than 'authentic experience'.

Dirk Bakker, CEO at Colliers International, the Netherlands, and Dessauvagie's colleague, offered up a similar view. He said: 'The average rate of an Airbnb room in most cities is almost at par with the average rate in a city. The difference is that you can stay in a hotel room with a maximum of two people, but in Airbnb you can stay in a room with four, five, six people, so per person it's cheaper and the majority [of people] book like that. It's not about the experience, it's about an accommodation that offers you a little bit more, gives you a bit more privacy, and price is a very important part of that.'

Colliers International was one of the groups to have contributed to the so-far slim volume of knowledge on the impact of Airbnb, driven by Bakker's loathing of the sound of wheeled suitcases trundling over the cobbles of Amsterdam, a noise synonymous for him with the sharing platform.

The company first sounded the alarm for falling rates in 2016, in a report alongside Colliers Hotelschool The Hague and AirDNA[14]. The report found that Airbnb had recorded 2 million overnight stays in London throughout 2015 and had seen the average daily rate (ADR) rise to $142 per night, compared to $220 for hotels in London. While Airbnb hosts recorded a total revenue of $286 million, hotels realised a total revenue of $8.1 billion in 2015.

A snapshot of January 2016 indicated that hotels saw year-on-year declines of 2 per cent in demand, 9 per cent in revenues and 5 per cent in occupancy. Over the same period, Airbnb saw 182 per cent growth in revenues, 126 per cent growth in occupancy and a 206 per cent increase in demand. The study said that: 'In the future, supply growth in Airbnbs in London is expected to be more limited than demand growth, in part

---

[14]www.colliers.com/en-gb/netherlands/insights/research/airbnb-londen. AirDNA gets, as the name suggests, to the very makeup of Airbnb and the sharing economy, providing data to the sector until that glorious time when Airbnb IPOs

driven by increased pressure from local governments and complaining neighbours for regulation, and from residents experiencing negativity when offering their property on the platform.'

Jeroen Oskam at Hotelschool The Hague, said[15]: 'London is the first place where we have detected an influence on hotels, whereas in Amsterdam both hotels and Airbnb have grown. In Amsterdam, we have warned people that the current boom in the hotel market may be concealing the influence of Airbnb. Most consultants up to now have been claiming that Airbnb is incremental, but this is not true. It is a low-cost option, with two and three stars most affected. I don't see the big hotel chains noticing that much impact, but it will affect the small, independent hotels.'

Marc Finney, head of hotels and resorts consulting at Colliers International, said: 'Airbnb has been regarded as a "disrupter" in the hotel industry for a number of years now and is said to have a major impact on the performance of traditional hotels, but until now there has been no publicly available data to support these claims. The hotels sector is strong in London, yet there's no doubt that the continued growth of Airbnb presents a threat. An interesting finding of the report is Airbnb's ability to perform even in the notoriously slow "off season". Our research showed that demand steadily increased throughout the year, and although we see a much faster increase in the summer months, this demand continues to increase outside of peak season. This demonstrates that Airbnb does not seem to be impacted by seasonality in the market place, which gives it a distinct advantage as this is not something that we are seeing as much in the hotels sector.'

HSBC, which also used AirDNA data, issued in a note that the operators it covered – Accor, InterContinental Hotels Group and Whitbread – were less impacted than previously thought, down to their exposure to budget accommodation and corporate business. It added: 'That said, we think the sheer volume of Airbnb supply in France puts Accor most at risk, with IHG next, and Whitbread most insulated given penetration in the UK is heavily skewed to London, where Premier Inn is competitively priced'.

The bank wasn't alone. Back in 2014, UBS had got out its long black cloak and scythe in a note in which it said that increased supply from shared accommodation was likely to affect the hotel industry, 'especially those hotels with a low business mix and which operate in the economy/ budget sectors'. It added: 'While we estimate 55 per cent of Whitbread clients travel for business and the company operates in the UK midscale and economy segment, we do not think they will be immune from some of the impact from shared accommodation.'

Looking back at that time, Frits van Paasschen[16], author, citizenM advisory board, and former Starwood Hotels & Resorts president and CEO, said: 'The reality is that Airbnb has been ascendant since the financial crisis. What I saw, even in my last two years at Starwood, in 2014, 2015, was record occupancies in the hospitality sector across North America and certainly robust RevPAR growth in Europe and most of Asia. What we have not yet seen is what the landscape of lodging looks like with Airbnb as a major player at the time of the downturn. Continuing to watch the market unfold – particularly in Europe where Airbnb is quite strong – and to see, at one point during my tenure, 40,000 listings across the city where there were maybe 100,000 or 110,000 business hotel rooms. That's an extraordinary amount of supply.

---

[16]And former Nike president of Europe, Middle East, and Africa, former Coors CEO. One of the few, like former IHG CEO Andy Cosslett, to come in from The Outside. One of his key moments in the sector was pursuing Hilton after an industrial espionage case that saw some of Starwood's documents relating to the W brand half-inched. The sector was shocked when van Paasschen pursued Hilton, leading to a ban on the group launching a boutique brand for two years. The usual punishment for such matters was a ducking in the pool at the IHIF conference in Berlin. Van Paasschen said: 'We had no choice but to stand up and protect our brands.' This was revolutionary thinking in 2010. No wonder he wrote a book about disruptors.

'What not everybody realises about that supply is that [Airbnb] has created for the first time in the history of the industry elastic supply in the short term. It used to be, if there were not enough rooms in the city, it would take a long time to build a hotel; in the meantime, the hoteliers would be enjoying the most fantastic rates. Now you have all these rooms which could come onto the market at peak periods of tourism, and suddenly the spikes in rates that you could get from having inelastic supply and growing demand aren't there like they used to be. I think Airbnb has had a dramatic effect and I don't think we know what a slowdown looks like with them in the marketplace. I think we're going to find the answer to both of those things in the next few years, because this cycle can't continue forever.'

As van Paasschen described, a growing conclusion had been that the sharing platforms were negatively impacting hotels on the nights in which hotels make most of their money: compression or constraint nights, when more than 95 per cent of rooms were occupied, allowing hotels to raise rates and profitability (PwC had a slightly more lyrical term for compression nights, calling them 'the cream of the milk'[17] when it warned that Airbnb could be feasting on the fat). The increased supply from Airbnb and chums was, it was felt, limiting the number of compression nights.

Data from STR suggested that the impact was not as great as feared. Looking at peak periods, in, for example, Paris in July, the company reported that compression nights had halved, from 10 to five between 2015 and 2018, but rates on those nights had risen by 9 per cent. The results varied according to seasonality.

STR's figures made a case for controlling the supply of Airbnb accommodation in New York, a city where the arguments between Airbnb, the city's politicians and its hotel companies had been raging

---

[17]www.pwc.co.uk/blogs/migrated/uk-hotels-forecast-2016.pdf

for some time to the delight of journalists but, as is sadly so often the case, the irritation of everyone trying to take a long-term view of the market. STR reported a solid increase in compression nights in the city of 20 per cent for the period between 2015 and 2018.

Bazin described the impact on the group, as customers told him that 'price mattered and it was very impactful on constraint days, those days when you have an airshow, when you have the World Cup, where we used to have 100 per cent occupancy … when you have 100 per cent occupancy it's a pretty good day because you can push through your own price. Those constraint days have been elapsing because Airbnb was adding supply and you had fewer and fewer constraint days and less and less advantage. That was impactful three or four years ago, less so today'.

Looking at the world as he saw it, Bazin added: 'Airbnb has been an impact mostly on the economy and midscale, but if you look at it now, you realise that 90 per cent of Airbnb clients are still users of hotel brands and hotel networks. And 50 per cent of Airbnb users would not have travelled without Airbnb existing. The hotel industry is very simple, it's mostly us – the big guys, two-thirds to 75 per cent B2B, corporate. On Sunday to Friday you have less than 1.5 person per room and it's 75 per cent of your business. That person coming for business, if he wants to go back to the same town with his buddies, or grandchildren, he's going to use Airbnb or Onefinestay because it's cheaper and more fun.'

Chappell was sceptical of the hit being taken by the global operators on these days, believing that convenience was behind some of the blame heading Airbnb's way and that it suited the sector to do so. 'If you're the CEO of a large, branded hotel company coming under pressure,' he said, naming no names, 'it's very convenient to point to Airbnb and say "Oh well, we're coming under pressure with these new disruptors in the marketplace" and I think it has been hard to give it credence. We work in the industry and it has been very hard to get good, reliable data on the impact of this, so I find it very hard to believe that the hotel brands and companies, smart as they are, have any access to any secret data that we don't, so they are operating from the same conjectures that we are. Do I think it's having an impact? No, I do not. I have never had the impression that hotel bookings and rates are down because people have decided to stay at an Airbnb-type product.'

Another explanation for the issues around constraint nights, Chappell said, was that consumers themselves were aware that hotels were taking liberties with their rates because they could, and so were voting with their heads – taking them off the pillow and just plain staying for shorter periods of time.

Hotels' fascination for driving ever-higher rates was something that mystified Andy Cosslett[18], IHG's CEO from 2005 to 2011, who joined the company not from decades working the floor at the world's hotels, but from Cadbury Schweppes, where, as he told this author, he was focused on selling more chocolate bars, not increasing the price of the bars themselves. The philosophy didn't really catch on in the hotel sector, although the idea of commoditising hotel rooms as one might a bar of Dairy Milk would certainly resonate with the OTAs once they had identified hotels as a marketable product that wasn't being marketed well.

It didn't do to be too cynical. Harper added that certain locations had far higher numbers of Airbnb offerings, which tended to increase the impact the segment has on hotel trading and values. Indeed, in many areas, an oversupply in Airbnb accommodation could lead to lower room rates being generated across the market. In Cancun, Mexico, for example,

---

[18]At the last sighting he was chairman of the Rugby Football Union and there's probably a correlation to be had to banging heads together there too.

he had seen room rates drop by almost 25 per cent in certain seasons because of the oversupply of Airbnb accommodation impacting on how the hotels can trade, with budget-conscious leisure travellers being wooed away from traditional hotel offerings.

Guy Parsons, CEO at easyHotel, agreed with Chappell and felt that the compression night argument itself was a touch of the lady protesting too much. He said: 'Far be it from me to be cynical, but that's just another excuse from hotels. Either the event is not producing the demand that it was or you have oversupply. We haven't seen that we're competing directly with Airbnb, except in Budapest – it's the only city where we can say that. And in Budapest it's an oversupply issue, there are just too many rooms available.'

Parsons' easyHotel operated at the 'superbudget-and-proud' end of the spectrum[19], which did not, unlike Travelodge and Premier Inn, go as far as to offer restaurants or swimming pools[20], but was a straight-to-the point no-frills offering, with a dash of orange, as one would expect. Parsons, who had been in the role since 2015, had a pedigree in the budget sector, having also been CEO at Travelodge and worked at both Travel Inn (the artist now known as Premier Inn) and Accor's Novotel brand, the original concept of which, Parsons said, 'was that you could walk into one and, even if you couldn't speak the language, you'd be able to identify where the lifts were, where the restaurant was, without asking people'. And more of how Accor has evolved its budget brands later.

Unlike Premier Inn and Travelodge, Parsons was confident that the peer-to-peer lodging sector wasn't eating off his plate, with a refreshing

---

[19]Obviously. Alongside easyPizza, easyGym, easyInternetcafe, easyMoney, easyCruise, easyMobile, easyCar and, alarmingly, easy4Men. If you're tempted to get on board this train, don't be – Stelios has many a successful court case under his belt after taking on those who would take Easy. Not so easy now, headline writers delighted.
[20]OK, in Dubai. Not Stoke.

grasp of what his brand offered. He said: 'People dwell for much longer in an Airbnb than they do in ours; where they arrive, drop bag, go. We can't cater for some of those people. Our rooms aren't big enough, we don't have the facilities. If someone is coming for a two-week holiday and they have massive suitcases, we don't have the luggage capacity – we haven't got the space in our rooms. That's not our offer. You're not going to one of our hotels because you're going to one of our hotels. You're going because you want to be in Berlin, or you want to be in a particular location. If you're going to Berlin for Airbnb, you may be there for longer, but you will certainly use it in a different way: to have dinner, invite friends round, use it in a completely different way than you use a hotel.'

Parsons pointed to the way that the sharing economy was becoming part of the hospitality mix with the next wave of travellers, commenting: 'If I look at my children's use of Airbnb, they use it in very different ways and they use both it and hotels. On the occasions where they want to use a hotel, it may just be a one- or two-night stay where they're looking for consistency and their primary focus is doing something else. You want a guarantee that the room is going to be there, it's going to be as advertised, all the things that the hotel guarantees. That's a really good reason to use a hotel and that's what we offer. Because we don't have swimming pools or restaurants, we're providing the base for people to do something else. We're very rigid about that, that's what we want to offer. The margins in hotels are better than in restaurants, that's exactly what our clientele wants.'

Premier Inn, when faced with constant questioning on the 'Airbnbers-like-it-cheap' thesis, took the 'fresh, new traveller' defence when considering Airbnb, while claiming no significant impact on performance. A popular argument in the sector, it looked to the idea that the guest in question would have stayed at home if no Airbnb were available. For those with long memories, the argument was much the same as that which serenaded the growth of the budget sector in the UK and led to the flourishing of Travelodges and Premier Inns in motorway service stations. Guests who would have couch-surfed or not stayed at all, we were told. Why must it always come back to sofas?

As a postscript to Whitbread's adventures with sharing, the company announced the trial of a super-budget brand, Zip, in 2018. Hey, if there's pie, why not grab a slice, right?

A more nuanced variant on the ideas of pies and cost came from Tim Ramskill, managing director, head of EMEA equity research, Credit Suisse, who saw the pie growing – backed up by the UNWTO[21], which reported that international tourist arrivals reached a total of 1.32 billion in 2017, up 7 per cent on the year and well above the organisation's long-term forecast of 3.8 per cent per year for the period 2010–2020. More demand would surely save hotels.

Ramskill said that, at the margin, peer-to-peer lodging made it slightly cheaper to stay in a city longer and might help to expand the market, but that it was principally new supply against a backdrop of an industry that enjoyed growth over the long term. Without demand booming, the sharing sector could be bad news but, as it stood, all parties had been able to ride the expansion upwards.

Bakker backed him up, describing a compounded annual growth rate of arrivals around the world of 7.4 per cent. Hotel construction's compounded annual growth rate, he said, was 4.4 per cent 'so that's where Airbnb has jumped in'.

Dessauvagie added reassurance, as a proper colleague does: 'The good thing is that when you look at a hotel investment, we always start with a sense of the hotel performance and the tourism numbers in a certain market and despite Airbnb and other platforms, hotel demand is still very

---

[21]www.e-unwto.org/doi/pdf/10.18111/9789284419876

much on the rise – and that's understating it. It's booming. That will attract hoteliers and hotel investors. We do get questions from our clients asking whether they should still be investing in Airbnb, but if you look at hotels, they are seeing higher results every year and we see that it won't have any effect on the investment business.'

For Ramskill, price was certainly a consideration when consumers were looking at Airbnb, not only in terms of cheapness, but in terms of value, with the sharing platform offering more social and communal space than an equivalent-priced hotel room. Ramskill pointed to efforts by hotels to develop more appealing communal space, but there was just no substitution for having your own social space to which nobody else was invited.

Commenting on the impact on the economy hotel sector – and pointing to the fact that, with Airbnb's guidance, amateur hosts could be professional revenue managers – Ramskill identified the platform's flexibility as its strength, with savvy hosts using it to bring their properties to the market at the right times to take advantage of spikes in supply, such as during sporting events. In other words, that cream that hotels used to like to skim off the top.

Van Paasschen cautioned against focusing too much on the price issues around peer-to-peer lodging, saying: 'Step back a moment and recognise that the pattern of disruption across industries is for disruptors to start at the low end and at the fringes of markets and work their way upmarket. People often think that innovation somehow comes from the high end, but most disruptive innovation starts at the low end in a way that's not really recognised by the incumbents, which is exactly what we saw with Airbnb. You see the same thing in steel minimills, Japanese automotives starting out as Datsuns and turning into Lexuses, so the real question isn't which Airbnb should the hotel companies be going after. The hotel companies should be recognising that Airbnb is coming into their market, and that the incremental traveller that they're taking into their system today, tomorrow might be going to an Airbnb listing, as that content becomes more predictive and more convenient and more reliable for business travellers who are spending more. Today, the overlap isn't there as it might be, but that overlap will continue to be a competitive threat to the traditional hotel companies.'

There was a case to be made that homesharing was itself creating demand. Kate Nicholls, CEO at UKHospitality, posited that the biggest competition faced by the hospitality sector was 'the sofa[22] and staying at home and not going out – whether that's restaurants, pubs, bars, clubs or hotels – so Airbnb was great at getting a new generation into the habit of going out on holiday and going on staycations. Eventually they would graduate up, eventually they will want to have a more luxurious, more sophisticated experience. Maybe they will still do Airbnb in certain cases where they want to feel more like a local, or where they want to have that more authentic experience. They'll get into the habit of doing two or three little trips a year and they'll use hotels as well.'

For those who would invest in the hotel sector, it was clear that there was competition to be had in the economy market, but could the sharing economy also be luring away guests who would otherwise have stayed in a hotel – maybe those heavy on gold, marble and flunkies? There was the suspicion that the branded hotel sector had it too good for too long, feeding on a customer who had become used to being told what they wanted and liking it. Those times, as retailers around the world have noted, were now past and tastes were changing, tastes that the sector was having issues keeping up with and that might have more to do with the experience of the sharing economy than price alone.

Criticisms of samey shopping malls had also landed at the door of the hospitality sector, which had become heavily branded. By 2019, STR was

---

[22]Possibly now is the time to call for a ban on sofas.

reporting that two branded hotels were opening for every unbranded hotel[23]. An after-dinner game whispered about in the sector but never played was one where photos of bedrooms were passed around hotel CEOs and they had to guess which brand they belonged to. Heads could roll[24]. Because in this era of brand proliferation, distinguishing features were not heavy on the ground. As Lennert de Jong, commercial director at citizenM[25], said: 'I wouldn't describe the brands under Marriott and Hilton as brands, they're just selection criteria.'

Bland had further words of caution about the likely effect of the peer-to-peer sector, describing it as 'polarising. It's pushing consumers towards either luxury or economy and it's leaving the poor old midscale hotel in something of a quandary because what's the point of it? If you've got money to spend on the experience, then you want something a little bit better. That has been, I think, a driver behind Accor's[26] acquisitions. They haven't bought that many midscale hotels, and economy hotels – they have plenty of them – so they bought Fairmont Raffles, they launched new brands that are funkier, edgier; they're not classic rivals to Ibis. That realisation that the generic midscale hotel is facing a challenge – I'm not going to say it's dead because there's always a market for something – but there is a realisation that there's a challenge and if you want to drive growth in distribution you have to offer something a little bit different.'

When trying to work out what Airbnb was, it was important not to be seduced by Airbnb's vision of itself as a helpmeet to Clarice from Dallas, who was using the platform to raise a few dollars to help fund her organic

---

[23]So the company's Robin Rossmann told IHIF 2019.

[24]In 2018, IHG patented a room design in the US. It had beds ON A SLANT.

[25]12 hotels around the world and a healthy pipeline with, as you may have guessed from de Jong's comments, just the one brand. Pioneers of the idea that guests might want to have a pleasant place to hang out that isn't alone in their room with warm gin.

[26]Seriously. Check your inbox, they're probably trying to buy you right now. In 2019, Bazin announced that the group was not going to do any more M&A (although he still wanted 50 brands). Observers believed him for no seconds.

scarf business (looms need rooms too). The company was very fond of heartwarming host profiles and its city impact studies became the canary for imminent strategy change – one released whenever the local authority started to narrow its eyes in the direction of sharing. Us hacks learned that when a report on how many small independent businesses in Paris were benefitting from homesharing landed in our inbox, a fresh assault on that city – or by that city – could not be far behind.

As we will see later, those listing on homesharing platforms were not all amateurs – sorry Clarice – but neither were they offering the cheapest possible stay, on a mattress pressed up against that loom. Airbnb was not immune to the luxury end of the market and, in 2018, to coincide with its 10th anniversary, it launched Airbnb Plus[27], offering 'only the highest-quality homes with hosts known for great reviews and attention to detail'.

Starting with 2,000 homes in 13 cities, all available to book right now, Airbnb Plus was intended, the platform said: 'for guests looking for beautiful homes, exceptional hosts and added peace of mind. Airbnb Plus homes have been inspected and verified in person against a 100+ point checklist covering cleanliness, comfort and design. Airbnb Plus hosts benefit from top placement, in-home services such as design consultation and expert photography, and premium support'. At a cost to hosts, of course, but the not-onerous $149 at launch.

As part of the 'roadmap to magical travel' the company also introduced Beyond by Airbnb, a travel service that offered curated experiences that included luxury accommodations as well as custom 'experiences', all of which was the product of Airbnb's acquisition of Luxury Retreats in 2017. The magical roadmap was designed to help Airbnb to 1 billion guests by 2028, and right about here you can insert all the comments you like about

---

[27]https://press.airbnb.com/airbnb-unveils-roadmap-to-bring-magical-travel-to-everyone/

the hotel sector needing to decide whether it was going to be a cowardly lion in its response to the threat.

The other issue facing the sector was that real estate investors were fickle beasts and relatively new to hotels. Hotels, unlike, say, sweatshops, required regular capex investment alongside the cost of buying the thing in the first place. Changes of allegiance were more than likely if yields were looking perkier elsewhere and, while hotels were commenting on the size of a pie big enough for all to feast on, others were still looking to increase their stake from delicious filling to crust, and some were starting to look at the sharing economy as a possible home for their cash – cash that those in the hotel sector grumbled could have been better placed building a nice new Radisson.

The first sign that homesharing was likely to make money for investors other than Ashton Kutcher was in 2018, when BNP Paribas Real Estate's property management business announced an agreement with professional homestay management company Hostmaker to offer a model for residential assets in Europe that mixed long-, medium- and short-term leases in a flexible way to optimise returns.

Csongor Csukás, head of international property management at BNP Paribas Real Estate, said: 'We observe significant interest among major real estate investors in the residential sector, as well as fast-growing trends in consumers' preferences such as nomadism, co-living, extra services and tailor-made user experience. Residential letting and property management is an extremely atomised sector with a clear opportunity for professional managers due to the lack of transparency and efficient management models. Combining tenants' experience, strategic PropTech partners and the technology, we bring value with branding, management, efficiency and long-term strategy.'

The product would include, it said, hands-off premium services that included: listings on platforms such as Airbnb (description, high-quality pictures), guest screening, hosting (in-person meet and greets, five-star housekeeping), and maintenance (fixing, interior design, etc.). For all residents, there would be enhanced experiences by bringing to them a range of premium services (including cleaning, home-staging, etc.). BNP Paribas Real Estate said it would 'enhance property value by setting up five-star standards'.

Nakul Sharma, CEO and founder of Hostmaker, said: 'This collaboration will provide BNP Paribas Real Estate customers with a one-stop shop service for property management. BNP Paribas Real Estate has long offered a range of lease management functions; Hostmaker will now supplement this by offering an innovative flexible lettings model, to increase occupancy rates, mitigate risk and increase yields.'

Paul Abrey, head of professional services, including property management, and board member in the UK, said that an investor might wish to consider several floors of a build-to-rent property for the Hostmaker offering, and pointed to the higher service cost of such a property, which could be offset by the potential for higher rent charged.

He added: 'Build-to-rent property at the top end is a digital experience, leasing it is a digital experience. The future is to have shared spaces, cinema rooms. I think that residents should be able to book cleaners daily, weekly, whenever they want, and they should be able to do it online.' When asked whether the move meant that the sharing economy was now an asset class, Abrey said: 'I wouldn't put it as an asset class, but the sharing economy and placemaking are definitely on every investor's agenda.'

This agenda was being aided by the higher returns coming from sharing against traditional residential letting. A study by Ortus Structured Finance[28] in February 2018, using data from Zoopla, found that the average rent for a one-bed flat in London was £1,618 a month, while a single private room on Airbnb could bring in around £100 per night, just

---

[28]http://ortussecuredfinance.co.uk/buy-let-landlords-turn-airbnb-style-lets-higher-yields/

as average rents across the UK began to shrink for the first time in five years towards the end of 2017.

Airbnb itself liked the idea of the property market so much – why should it just be Clarice who benefits? – that at the start of 2018, Brookfield Property Partners confirmed that it was to invest up to $200 million in a joint venture with Niido, the multifamily development partner of Airbnb.

Jaja Jackson, director, global multifamily housing partnerships, Airbnb, said: 'This partnership shows how landlords, developers and Airbnb can work together to create value for everyone and better serve tenants. The team at Newgard is leading the way and we're thrilled to work with them. Together, we're making it easier for more hosts to share their space, and giving guests access to more affordable options when they travel.'

Tenants would have permission to rent their homes on Airbnb for up to 180 days per year, giving their landlord a portion of the earnings. The apartments were designed with the sharing economy in mind, with keyless entry, shared common spaces and a 'master host' at each property, who can assist with cleaning rooms or checking guests in.

Chris Lehane, Airbnb's global head of policy and public affairs, said: 'This is going to be part of the future of housing, not only in Florida, but also across the country.' For Airbnb, the move gave it some control over its supply in a market where regulation had ebbed and flowed globally, in a manner that must be pretty irritating if you're trying to get an IPO off the ground. While the hotel sector had complained about transparency as rooms came on and off the market at the will of the hosts, for Airbnb the other side of this sword was that it had no supply guarantees with its hosts either.

The platform also undertook a test in Paris with Century 21, which it said would make it 'easier to sublet'. Under the terms of the agreement, any tenant or landlord whose contract has been entered into with Century 21 may apply for an Airbnb-friendly lease, which authorises subletting as part of a revenue share between the landlord, tenant and agency. It is worth noting that Paris was one of the platform's biggest markets and one where the local law had been most vociferous in its feelings about the platform. Given that the French have a habit of taking their issues out on to the street, any strategy was worth a shot. It may not get to the dung-throwing state of the farmers in 2014, but that's not a risk those in the Hôtel de Ville thought was worth taking.

Many landlords were looking to tap into this market by obtaining funding to increase their current property portfolio or convert existing assets. Research from the Residential Landlord Association[29] in the UK showed that the number of buy-to-let investors renting on Airbnb saw a 54 per cent increase between February 2016 and March 2017, according to a survey of 1,463 landlords, with an 8 per cent increase in the number of these listings that are available for more than 90 nights per year. This meant, it said, a potential 12,213 homes unavailable for families to rent for the long term. In the same period, the RLA said that 7 per cent of landlords were now moving properties from long-term to short-term lets.

And it was these concerns that piqued the interest of governments around the world – with the potential to limit not only the number of properties available through homesharing, but also their profitability. The hotel sector rejoiced.

'I fought the law but the law kept changing the rules of engagement' – in which hotels look to legislation to fight sharing

An Englishman's home might be his castle but have you ever tried heating one recently? As Clarice in Dallas may have found, renting out the sofa

---

[29]https://research.rla.org.uk/wp-content/uploads/Is-Airbnb-becoming-the-new-buy-to-let-Residential-Landlords-Association-August-2017.pdf

could help put food on the table and, as Bland put it: 'I can't imagine that if you're particularly reclusive and hated people that [being a host] would appeal to you for a minute'. Why not monetise your personal strengths and your real estate? You've eaten baked beans for a decade to get on to that bottom rung of the housing ladder, so what you do with that castle is your own business, from what colour you paint it, to who sleeps on the pull-out bed. There was an argument for homesharing that focused hard on sharing and harder on the freedom of the homeowner.

Except not. It turned out that being part of society came with certain rules, and making it harder for others to get on to that rung – because investors were turning to short-term lets to make money and pushing up housing prices – was bad. Worse still, taking housing out of the loop altogether was very bad. Blaming one part of the market for its failings was also bad, but this hadn't slowed down a number of jurisdictions from identifying the homesharing market as the source of all the ills of society.

Initially, when Airbnb materialised (and for 'initially', read this as 'once Airbnb had hit 3 million listings' – most of the hotel industry having refused to notice the elephant in the room until it was wearing gold tassels and bedecked in acrobats, PT Barnum-style), hotels responded to these dawning millions of rooms by falling back on the idea that, 'well, who doesn't like, and wouldn't continue to like, hotels?', but also that someone in a judge's black robes would protect them with a soothing barricade of laws banning it outright.

Giving double the hope to a hotel sector eager to get legislators to do their dirty work, the cities most quick to react to homesharing were also those where overtourism had started to be a feature of daily life, cities where the locals found themselves becoming living attractions, but without seeing much benefit from the ticket price. Just the kind of city in which hotels liked to be, too.

And science seemed to back this up. A 2016 study by researchers at the University of Siena concluded that sharing platforms were changing the face of the country's historic cities. *The Airification of Cities* report[30] said: 'The three larger cities frequently recurring in the touristisation discourse – Florence, Venice, Rome – all have a proportion of their centres' housing stock on Airbnb above 8 per cent. This figure could be considered a sort of canary value for the Disneyfication of the centre. Cities approaching it should seriously reflect on whether touristisation and Disneyfication are desirable conditions for their historical centre. Population has been lost, and city residents increasingly tend to perceive these areas with a certain detachment, as no longer belonging to their daily experience of the city. This is a phenomenon that pre-dates Airbnb by far, but the availability of Airbnb data allows us to effectively visualise part of the dynamics at play.

'In typical Italian fashion, there has been very little debate over the long-term consequences of a relatively new phenomenon, especially one associated with novelty, entrepreneurialism and "new" technologies, and the only intervention that the government has deemed necessary has been that of imposing a tax on homes rented through the platform.'

Van Paasschen was willing to spread the net of blame wider, with the idea that: 'I don't think Airbnb is the cause of overtourism, but they're certainly a partner in overtourism – as are hotel companies and tour companies and cruise lines. I don't think there's a single cause of overtourism, other than there are some really great places to go, and there's an increasing prosperity in both time and money so that people can go to those places; how we navigate that is an important thing that we in the industry have to think about. Will there be a backlash against Airbnb in the context of that? There already has been and I think that is a reality of overtourism and what it does to indigenous communities.

'I don't think there's a simple solution, individual cities have to look at different ways to spread out tourist traffic. There's always an economic

---

[30]http://ladestlab.it/maps/73/the-airification-of-cities-report

incentive to bring in tourists and tourism is a great industry as long as it doesn't spoil the locations where there are so many tourists, so how do you find ways to make certain locations more expensive, or less accessible for waves of tourism, or how do you spread out where people go in a city – do you move museums? I think there will be attempts at solutions but it's not obvious as to how we're going to make a serious dent in overtourism.'

Eager to find these solutions, and quickly, in 2018 Airbnb launched the Office of Healthy Tourism[31], which it hoped would address the issue. In addition to the office, Airbnb said that it would release data 'that shows the benefits of healthy tourism for hosts, guests, and cities around the world', as well as creating a Tourism Advisory Board, which would be made up of travel industry leaders from around the world.

The board included David Scowsill, CEO, Eon Reality and former president and CEO at the World Travel & Tourism Council (WTTC), who said: 'One billion more people will be in the global middle class by 2030, and these new entrants will be looking to travel to enhance their horizons. The concentration of tourism in key locations is creating a threat to their future, by causing congestion, overcrowding, and a deteriorating quality of life for residents. Spreading the tourists around each city and each country geographically is an important step to solving this overcrowding problem.'

Lehane said: 'With travel and tourism growing faster than most of the rest of economy, it is critical that as many people as possible are benefiting – and right now not all tourism is created equal. To democratise the benefits of travel, Airbnb offers a healthy alternative to the mass travel that has plagued cities for decades. Airbnb supports tourism that is local, authentic, diverse, inclusive and sustainable. Through the meaningful income earned by the mosaic that is our global

---

[31]www.airbnbcitizen.com/airbnb-launches-global-office-of-healthy-tourism-2/

community of hosts, our ability to promote tourism to places that need it the most, and the inherent sustainable benefits of hosting, Airbnb is providing the type of travel that is best for destinations, residents and travellers alike.'

The company's first act was to sign a memorandum of understanding with the government of Jujuy, Argentina, aimed at promoting tourist activity in rural towns and natural areas; helping jujeños open their homes to travellers from all over the world through the platform, exchanging aggregated tourism data and collaborating in disaster situations.

Without wishing to dismiss an idea out of hand – other than putting in turnstiles in Venice, an effort that lasted for one whole day before residents tore them down – no one was going to visit Jujuy until they had ticked St Mark's Square off the list.

Bakker acknowledged this: 'Of course people want to come to Amsterdam. Amsterdam has the name, you'll never stop that'. He pointed to work by the local government to push visitors and the hotels they would stay in outside the city to the surrounding areas. He pointed to efforts made in Haarlem to promote it as a destination, branding Amsterdam's surroundings, and drawing off some of the heat, commenting: 'There are so many historic cities in the Netherlands that today don't have so much tourism, but which would be very interesting for Chinese and for Americans and others as well. That has already started and it will accelerate. The Internet provides the opportunity to make everything visible through nice pictures and easy clicks to encourage people to go to other places; at the end of the day, if you've been to Amsterdam and you can't properly walk and you can't find a hotel because hotels are so damn expensive, then you will go elsewhere. It's already happening as you can see from hotel development and prices in cities like Utrecht and Haarlem.'

This hadn't passed Airbnb by and the platform announced plans to divert part of its €5 million Community Tourism Programme into support areas across the Netherlands that were 'suffering from undertourism'[32]. The platform said: 'The Netherlands is a wonderful country with a diverse range of regions and we are already witnessing how the Airbnb platform is helping guests to experience the country as a local and discover new places, previously inaccessible to them. In 2017, over half of the communities in the Netherlands with an active listing on Airbnb had no hotel and three out of four guests said they chose Airbnb to visit a specific area.'

Bakker was working on that.

The hospitality sector as a whole was riding the growth of tourism, but had very little power to wield when it came to saying who travelled where. Not building a hotel in Venice was a matter for planners, given that hotel CFOs were unlikely to take a moral argument as an excuse for passing on a slam dunk.

Amsterdam was one city quick to act and, before the sharing platforms raised a rumpus, it had been 'equal opportunities' in terms of its efforts, placing a moratorium on new hotels in the city centre and focusing on business guests rather than leisure travellers. One's thoughts turn to Bakker in this situation: 'I can't even ride my bike any more, it's a total mess – there are so many tourists'.

For the sharing economy, this meant a series of agreements signed with the city's authorities, beginning in 2015, when Airbnb agreed to collect local taxes from those renting through their site, and remit them to the city. Under the agreement, Airbnb hosts were presented with clear information about the rules of private renting in the city, which Airbnb promoted prominently, and with which the hosts had to declare they had complied, prior to making a listing. Airbnb then started collecting a 5 per cent tourist tax from hosts, to pass back to the city.

---

[32] www.airbnbcitizen.com/airbnb-launches-fund-to-support-areas-in-the-netherlands-suffering-from-undertourism/. What a thing to suffer from, 'undertourism'. It's all so very Goldilocks. If only we could get it just right.

'This is good news for our hosts, who will benefit from a simplified tourist tax process, and clearer information on what local laws and regulations may apply to them,' said Airbnb in a statement. 'It is also a great example of how we are working together with policy makers across the world on progressive rules that strengthen cities and help local residents make a little extra money to afford living costs.'

The agreement was followed by similar signings in Paris, London, Berlin, LA, New York, Tokyo and many points in between. The most common agreement was one that required not only tax, but also a limitation on listing, be that by type of listing or by time. In New York, only one active entire home listing in the city was allowed. In London, owners could not let property for more than 90 days in a given year on a short-term let. If an owner wanted to let for longer, they had to seek planning permission for change of use.

At the end of 2018, Airbnb – which, eyes to its IPO, had more incentive than most to act as the friendly player[33] – declared that it had partnered with more than 400 governments around the world to collect and remit taxes, and had collected and remitted more than $1 billion in travel and tourism taxes to date[34].

Bazin said that the impact of legislation had been to the benefit of Accor's constraint rates, although for him, as an industry player, 'I would never, ever seek protection from legislation'. Bazin instead described the move of Airbnb 'from capital cities, to secondary, tertiary cities, resort cities. What they have lost in gateways they have gained in smaller locations'.

Airbnb's world tour of tax agreements was not enough to satisfy those who were unable to exercise the cycling rights in cities such as Amsterdam,

---

[33]In 2018 in France, a voluntary commitment by the National Home Holidays Association – which includes Airbnb, HomeAway and TripAdvisor – was made, including measures such as asking their hosts to specify whether they rent a primary residence, a second home or a professional type of accommodation. Airbnb was quick to throw its rivals under the bus, commenting that the agreement would 'effectively combat bad actors'.

[34]www.airbnbcitizen.com/airbnb-collects-landmark-1-billion-in-hotel-and-tourism-taxes/

where Bakker described a city where it was not just the residential component that was changing but the city itself. 'Shops, garbage guys, they are changing their patterns in the cities due to neighbourhoods that change every day. The housing corporations, more than half are saying we don't want you to do Airbnb, city governments are clamping on people renting out their houses, so social housing – which used to be 44 per cent in Amsterdam – is no longer allowed to use Airbnb. If you are caught, there are huge deterrents. The periods when you can rent out your house on Airbnb have become much shorter. In Amsterdam it went from three months to two to one in the city centre.'

Legislation has not taken much of a toll on the growth of Airbnb. Between 2016 and 2018, its share of the overnight stay market increased by up to 3.4 per cent[35], according to Colliers International and Hotelschool The Hague, where the research found that the platform continued to grow in five main European cities – London, Amsterdam, Berlin, Madrid and Paris. London was the largest market for overnight Airbnb stays (6,703,337 overnight stays – a 45 per cent rise compared to the year before), just ahead of Paris (6,449,404 overnight stays – a 28 per cent rise from 2016/17), but the UK's capital was growing at a much faster rate.

Damian Harrington, head of EMEA research at Colliers International, said: 'Several cities have introduced legislation for Airbnb over the past few years. In Berlin, hosts were prohibited from offering an entire home on the platform since May 2016. In London, a rule was introduced that enabled hosts to let out their home for a maximum of 90 days per year. Similar legislation was introduced in Amsterdam, but here the maximum number of nights was limited to 60. Although the data can't clearly state whether hosts adhered to these rules, it does show that none of these cities were able to limit Airbnb growth in their respective cities. Madrid and

---

[35]www.colliers.com/en-gb/uk/insights/property-news/2018/0614-airbnb-legislations-do-little-to-dampen-growth-in-five-european-cities

Paris have announced that legislation will be introduced, but the effect of the new regulations is questionable.'

Amsterdam was, at the last sighting, considering banning Airbnb from some areas entirely, blaming it for stressing facilities and pushing up house prices. Bakker said: 'Housing prices are going up and from what we've seen in Amsterdam – ridiculously so. A lot of these semi-commercial owners of buildings have been buying up houses, splitting them up into apartments and renting them out as Airbnb.'

And it was this move into the commercial that sparked the ire of all involved. Nicholls said: 'You don't need new laws, you just say, "You're a commercial accommodation provider, you need to do the same thing as any commercial accommodation provider". They need to be in a certain use class. The existing legitimate suppliers have no problem with that – with statutory registration or any of the other requirements. That's the most important thing to learn about all these different spaces – digital is actually no different from the traditional businesses, but it is disruptive and it is a disruptor, but that's all it is. The issues to do with Facebook, Twitter, etc. are to do with data, confidentiality, transparency and what you are doing with customer data. And that transfers across to the Airbnbs and the OTAs, who have controlled the data. Look at the parallels – Facebook is a publisher, Deliveroo is a marketer. There are existing laws to deal with them. A lot of it just slots naturally into place, so rather than treating this as a new quirky type of company which is little and slick and homespun, we should treat it differently.

'Customers have got used to being able to do homeshare, they like it when they go away on holiday. On the other side, when they are letting out their own rooms when they go on holiday, they are using it to pay rent or to pay for some treats. It's not going to go away and the government also has an interest in embracing new technologies and wanting them to flourish. What we need to do is not treat bricks-and-mortar entrepreneurs less favourably than online entrepreneurs. We need to stop thinking about it in terms of the cuddly sharing economy and we need to accept that this is a commercial enterprise and tax it accordingly, and then it will find its own level in the marketplace.

'When you're looking at future regulation and asking how, if you can, you put the genie back into the bottle, it's about differentiating between those who are genuinely true to that original model versus those people who are commercial landlords and it's just a transaction. That's commercial exploitation, and that's when you let the customer down.'

As Bakker said: 'It has to be above board and it has to be taxed, and once that happens it becomes a lot less interesting for a lot of people.'

Van Paasschen pointed to the hell-you-might-as-well aspect of the sharing economy, where, unlike pulling a hotel out of the ground, the lack of investment required to put a room on the market added flexibility. He said: 'One of the interesting things about the sharing economy, whether that be Uber or Airbnb or even the gig economy overall, is that you're making assets available that are otherwise lying fallow. A night of lodging is a very perishable commodity, in that if you don't sell that room tonight, then that room for that night does not exist any more.

'The lower end of what is still profitable for people in a peer-to-peer environment is very different to what investors would be expecting for hotels for which they have paid a lot of money, not only to build or buy, but to maintain or staff. What will be interesting is, yes, I think that peer-to-peer lodging prices will go up with tax parity, but I think that in a downturn you will see peer-to-peer lodging finding it easier to get further towards the bottom than a hotel might.'

Bakker's belief that interest would wane once hosts had to pay tax and buy smoke detectors was an area where the hotel sector was showing a great deal of interest and where phrases like 'level playing field' meant paying the same taxes and adhering to the same costly red tape as the hotel sector – and seeing the hit on profitability accordingly. Nicholls said: 'You will inevitably find that when you regulate it and tax it you slow the supply and some of those commercial landlords who are really exploiting it will stop and return to commercial letting. The competition that you've got there, with those commercial landlords, is with residential, it's not with hotels. That's why we need to regulate it proportionally. I think you will see a reduction in certain places [after tax, etc.], although it depends on the location. In London, Airbnb listings are equivalent to a third of the hotel stock. It's only 16–17 per cent in Manchester and Liverpool.

'If you ensure that there's no tax incentives and no disproportionate regulation, then the homesharing model, the apartment model, the hotel model at all levels, has its own space in the marketplace. But the problem at the moment is that you have one area which is completely unregulated – in a lot of jurisdictions they don't know whether an apartment exists, so they can't know whether they are being safe or not. It's the unfair competition that people are concerned about, because the only reason that some of those stays are cheaper is because they're not subject to the same level of regulation.'

To the credit of many in the sector, there had been a shift in favour of taking the fight to the platforms. John Wagner, director at Cycas Hospitality[36], said: 'I want to compete on a fair basis; I'll hold my own to compete, if it's fair. If somebody doesn't have to pay taxes, doesn't have to pay attention to zoning laws, planning, health and safety laws, it's not fair. It's also not right. One of the negatives of Airbnb is that it's not really a level playing field with those of us in the mainstream hotel business. We have taxes to pay, we have regulations to adhere to, zoning

---

[36] 5,850 rooms and suites at 31 December 2018, across a number of brands, including Moxy and Residence Inn. The company is part of a wave of 'brand agnostic' groups who look for the best-fit flag for each site, something guaranteed to give the operators the yips and lead to an arms race in beauty parades with, we fear, both swimsuit and talent rounds.

permissions to get, health and safety things to get. That is a bit unfair if you're competing for the same customer grouping, so the advent of extra regulations makes it a more fair comparison and it's good for the traveller and good for us.'

But would the customer follow when prices rise? Dessauvagie thought so. 'In the long term, people will stick with Airbnb because a price increase won't come all at once and if Airbnb professionalises their platform more, particularly if they deal with fire regulations and those issues, people will be willing to pay more. One of Airbnb's great assets is its technical aspect: they have a very easy and accessible website which attracts a lot of people and now that they're offering more and more on that website I think that will only continue to grow. They are becoming more and more of a platform for travel and that will lead them to have a lasting impact on the tourism business. Because of that, even when they increase their prices, people will still come to them.

'It is their goal to become an eco-system for travel and they have great willpower to do that, and I think they will get there, too. I expect that Airbnb will change their business model in such a way that they will co-operate with the local governments. They can't keep up with fighting all the municipalities about different rules all the time and that can't last forever. At some point they will learn to work with the different municipalities and one of the ways to do that is to focus on different business models. So Airbnb is introducing services – loyalty, trips, the business segment – and they are working more towards being a disruptor to the OTAs. In the end it will be combination of Airbnb shifting their business model so that they can adhere more to local regulations, and it will mean better regulations in the future too.'

Everyone's sense of fairness would appreciate a level playing field, but who would be the referee? For Nicholls, it was a global issue, with 'a lot of jurisdictions comparing notes and realising that they need an international solution, rather than them going alone. Different ways of controlling it will be very local, because the legislative framework is very different, in terms of planning restrictions and controls. Data and planning and tax are going to be the big things, which people want to do at an international level, but at the moment the legislators aren't talking to each other. We need to share information on what's working and how it could work elsewhere, or what they've tried and has failed. What's happened to Google and Facebook? They mushroomed and now people are trying to bring in digital taxes. They were a case study in how they can't be trusted to do it themselves. So let's not do the same thing with these emerging technologies and put the framework in place now. Then the ultimate solution will be determined locally.'

One of the issues that became clear after Berlin placed a limit on homesharing was that hosts were merely switching their listings from one platform to another as they used up their time allocation, sometimes with the help of professional management companies. A simple switch of platform was possible because no one was looking.

John Webber, head of rating at Colliers International, worked with hotels in the UK to help them claim lower business rates by proving the impact of homesharing on their performance. He found himself hindered by resources and by the issue of being able to track where homesharing was taking place. He said: 'The disadvantage with a hotel where you're a Hilton or a Travelodge is that it's very easy, physically, for the Valuations Office to track them down. The chances of the VO picking up your next-door neighbour as an Airbnb within six months of that happening are very slim. This is down to two things: one is the visibility and two is the resources. The other element to it as well, which is where I think the playing field will not be level, is the fact that many of these Airbnb facilities will get small business relief, the value of them will be below the threshold of £15,000.

'The way that this government and previous governments have operated is to give concessions to people who work in a small business environment, whereas your Hilton or your Travelodge would never get that. Airbnb will continue to benefit from this, because the government has taken the view that every small retailer has got a vote, whereas M&S is just M&S. It's as cynical as that.

'Airbnbs, if they are being operated by small businesses, will tend to operate in a more advantageous way, not only because, once they are captured and found, they will be getting relief, but because they will probably never capture all of them. The VO could quite easily find all the Airbnb locations, but what they then have to do is go out and check, look at them, probably measure them and then enter them into the ratings list. The reality is that they won't have the resources to do that. Whereas going and identifying a Travelodge is much easier.

'The reality is that if you were running a billing authority as a private business, you would start to say "actually, we can do an exercise here by finding all these properties", but you would need to employ somebody to do all that and that's normally where they fail. They can't employ more people. It takes resources and it's short-sighted. The whole economy, all of these things are changing, but the VOs are set in their ways, they don't tend to keep up with what's happening in the real world and there's a laziness with what they have done. The VOs don't tend to keep up with what's going on in the real world in any sensible way and that's the real danger. Airbnb is something which is growing and growing, and the way that buildings are changing is also growing.'

Nicholls was looking to simple pressure on resources to motivate governments and local authorities to find the cash to fund investigations. She said: 'In the UK, I suspect what will drive it is concern about local authority funding, particularly around destination management and tourism. As we've got more austerity, the amount of money that's available for local marketing comes under pressure and they need to look at how to find it.'

Many who would have homesharing find a place and then get put in it were looking to regulation to which the hotel sector already had to adhere: fire and life safety. Of course, for every case of food poisoning through an accidental egg sandwich left out by a sharing host, one only has to look at the hotel sushi buffet, one of the great dangers of modern life[37]. But those level playing fields are in operation here, too.

Nicholls said: 'It's about protecting the consumer – it's the consumer that's at risk. If it's a genuine residential let, the local authorities have powers to deal with it. If there are lots of people staying in a premises, you have regulations for "Houses of Multiple Occupation", where they can make sure that people are safe, where they can make sure that fire regulations apply and people can get out. If you don't know where half of these flats are, in a two-bedroom flat you've got four people staying, or 12 people staying, that causes problems for the fire authorities and the police authorities. You can't make sure that those people are safe.'

Parsons added: 'Safety is their Achilles' heel: the first time there's a fire and somebody can't get out, or if there's a Me Too moment across clientele in Airbnb. It's a little like Uber – there were a number of assaults in London and they've had to do something about that, but there were a lot of people who felt something like that was happening with Uber before those cases came to light, too. I'm not saying that's happening with Airbnb, but if you wonder how can the model go wrong, it will because of having a non-regulated accommodation provider. The hotels have sprinkler systems and CCTV, and that will be the moment when the hotel industry will be able to say "you can stay with us because…".'

---

[37]Thoughts also turn to the Dominique Strauss-Kahn defence, whereby you can complain about the danger faced by guests in unregistered homesharing properties, but even a hotel can't protect against members of the French political hierarchy.

At the time of writing, Airbnb had no fire safety rules for its hosts, although it did offer hosts one free fire detector. It has also partnered with the American Red Cross[38] to offer some fire safety tips, including having an emergency plan and how to contact local emergency services.

HomeAway also offered a series of tips, including: 'If you are ever concerned for your safety or have an emergency, you should immediately leave the property and call 9-1-1'[39]. Vrbo also had tips[40] and Onefinestay[41] reminded hosts that: 'you will be responsible for ensuring that the Property is tidy and sufficiently clean and complies with all relevant Health & Safety Regulations'.

Not, the hotel sector was wont to point out, the same level of regulations to which they were subject, which in the UK included an emergency plan, fire doors, trained staff, fire alarms, emergency lighting and fire extinguishers. In England and Wales, a breach of fire regulations could lead to an unlimited fine and/or prison.

The issue of safety was also one that was slowing corporate travellers from embracing homesharing. Not, perhaps, so much on the part of the travellers themselves[42], but on the part of employers eager not to pay out should anyone be injured by, or because of, the hosts. Bazin said: 'There is no one using Airbnb for business trips alone. Airbnb is 90 per cent Business to Consumer [B2C], which is why we cross each other. They are trying to get into corporate, and they might one day get there. But think about an employer sending their people to an Airbnb, when they have absolutely no insurance cover when it comes to security hazards, hygiene,

---

[38]www.airbnb.co.uk/trust/home-safety

[39]https://help.homeaway.com/articles/What-are-some-fire-safety-tips-when-staying-at-a-property

[40]www.vrbo.com/discoveryhub/tips-and-resources/improve-performance/fire-safety-for-your-vacation-rental

[41]https://web.onefinestay.com/uk-host-terms-conditions/

[42]One US company quickly rescinded its enthusiasm for the sharing platform after realising that it increased the chances of employees fraternising when on drunken conference trips.

anything. If you send your people to my hotel and something happens, I'm on the hook. They will surely move more into B2B [Business to Business] but I am stepping more on their toes, so I'm fine.'

Airbnb faced its first real test on Hallowe'en 2019, when five people were shot dead in a house rented through the platform, in California. CEO Brian Chesky said that the platform was 'banning party houses' following the deaths, announcing a dedicated rapid response team. The platform also planned to verify every listing by the end of the year, to establish that hosts were who they said they were, that photos and information were accurate and that locations met safety standards. In an email to employees, Chesky said: 'The world moves at the speed of trust, and the more trust that exists, the more access we can all have. Airbnb is founded on trust, and our vision depends on us continuing to increase this in our community.'

Could have Airbnb prevented it? It's unlikely. Any house has the potential to become a party house, much as any parent can be fooled by the protestations of a child that homework is front of mind while planning a weekend away. There is one clear way in which Airbnb could ensure, pretty much, that party houses were a thing of the past and that would be to return to the old school, homespun ways of its inception and offer only properties which are shared with the host. Only when Airbnb opens the books ahead of its move into the public eye in 2020 will we know the true makeup of the platform and only then will we see the likely impact of forcing the hosts to stay onsite and actually host.

The 'come out, come out, wherever you are' of the sharing economy was something where homesharing stood accused, most loudly in New York, where the platforms, led by Airbnb, fought long and with more vengeance than has been seen elsewhere in the globe, which those of us observing could only attribute to the adversarial and litigious culture in the US. In the city that never sleeps, Airbnb battled around the clock with lawmakers to protect the identities of its hosts and their properties from being revealed, with some success.

The law kicked back in 2018, requiring that homesharing companies supply lists of information about their hosts to the authorities in the city. Airbnb responded: 'We're not surprised the City Council refused to meet with their own constituents who rely on homesharing to pay the bills and then voted to protect the profits of big hotels. The fix was in from the start and now New Yorkers will be subject to unchecked, aggressive harassment and privacy violations, rubber stamped by the City Council.'[43] One man's aggressive harassment is, of course, another's legitimate registration of a business.

Airbnb, working in concert with HomeAway, managed to call a temporary halt to the implementation of the law. The judge in New York, Paul A. Engelmayer, wrote: 'The compelled production from home-sharing platforms of user records is an event that implicates the Fourth Amendment [protecting against unlawful search or seizure]. The city has not cited any decision suggesting that the governmental appropriation of private business records on such a scale, unsupported by individualised suspicion or any tailored justification, qualifies as a reasonable search and seizure.'

Engelmayer went on to write that he did not feel that the hotel sector, including homesharing, needed strict regulation, with such measures more suited to industries such as firearms and alcohol. He wrote: 'The hotel industry does not involve inherently dangerous operations or have a history of pervasive regulation.'

The judge defended the rights of privacy for both hotels and hosts, writing: 'Like a hotel, a home-sharing platform has at least two very good reasons to keep host and guest information private, whether as to these users' identities, contact information, usage patterns, and payment practices. One is competitive: keeping such data confidential keeps such information from rivals (whether competing platforms or hotels) who

---

[43]https://techcrunch.com/2018/07/18/new-law-forces-airbnb-open-its-books-to-new-york-authorities/

might exploit it. The other involves customer relations: keeping such data private assuredly promotes better relations with, and retention of, a platform's users.'

For governments – sadly for both homesharing platforms and hotels – the focus was on the consumer. As Nicholls noted, guests kind of liked Airbnb. They did, however, also like having somewhere to live when they weren't on holiday and preferred that it be reasonably priced. This – unfortunately for governments – fell into its purview and was more complex than simply shrieking at the homesharing platforms, fun though that undoubtedly was.

Airbnb could, as Nicholls pointed out, take some of the hit: 'If you go back to what Airbnb started out as being, renting a room out in your house while you are there, you are the host. There are undoubtedly lots of people who are doing that in order to subsidise their rent, because rent levels are so high, and the rent levels are so high because so many people are on Airbnb. We need to get that balance right, otherwise we've got real challenges when it comes to managing the needs of the local populations in certain hotspots. At the moment it's where you've got those short-term lets that you have the issues. You need the planning regime to step in so that we can put self-catering units in a separate use class so that we can have control of how much there is in a certain jurisdiction.'

As Jeremy Kelly, director of global research at JLL, said[44]: 'The trend towards Airbnb has opened up a whole can of worms for local authorities – it has affected not only hotels but also residential, and there is now greater awareness of the need for affordable housing. You can see that local governments are taking development more seriously. The different styles of property are blurring, which is making it difficult for them to get a handle on.'

---

[44]*Hotel Analyst*, 6 September 2017

The issue of how to maintain enough housing stock in the major global cities so that people, and not just oligarchs, could live there may not be a conversation for these pages, although it is very much a debate for those who would seek to maintain supply of accommodation at the various sharing platforms, particularly those on the public markets. The first thing that shareholders were likely to want to see in a publicly listed company was constant, raging, unfettered, gloriously over-the-top quarter-on-quarter growth. It was the search for this kind of growth that led the likes of Uber and Facebook into practices that would get you struck off most Christmas card lists – the Attorney General's springs to mind – and Airbnb was to receive at least some plaudits for looking to put its house, if not all of its 6 million properties, in order.

The requirement for ever-greater supply could be seen in deals such as that with Brookfield Property Partners, but buildings took time to get out of the ground; much better that they already exist. Mark Essex, director, public policy, KPMG, cautioned that there was scope for a clash between what the house-dwelling public wants in terms of holidays and what it needs in terms of a roof, which was where governments are required to provide guidance. 'The government,' he says, 'has got to make rental work better, because at the moment you have social housing, which is indefinite tenure – but only if you pass the magic tests – you have owner/occupation, which is indefinite tenure unless they put a train through it, and in between you have six months if you're lucky, unless the landlord wants to sell. You can't put a kid into school on a six-month tenancy – where's the stability? They're going to have to make rental tenures longer and if they do that it is less supply for Airbnb, not more.'

Essex was more than just a provider of problems, not solutions, ferreting out a cunning way to make sharing behave more like caring and something that, frankly, we should all have thought of earlier: people power. Essex said: 'It's a new disruption and legislation hasn't kept up, so we've had to rely on pressure from neighbours and peers to try and get these businesses to meet their obligations not to disturb the neighbours – just like hotels can't.'

The hotel sector and local authorities complained about the issue of knowing where homesharing sites were located, lacking as they were in signage other than lockboxes for keys. But local residents also found that they must come to terms with an element of surprise they hadn't bargained for, either when moving house or waking up one morning (or one 3am) to discover their neighbours have gone all entrepreneurial. Nicholls said: 'You've moved into a place with the belief that you were moving into a residential area, then you find yourself living next to a hotel. If that was licensed, a local authority would be able to close it down. If you moved next door to a pub, it's your own fault – but equally, if that pub was causing a nuisance, then you would be able to complain.'

In Amsterdam, a certain grating on the nerves was starting to be felt, if not yet acted upon by guests. Dessauvagie described an increase in resistance to Airbnb, thinking of it as akin to smoking cigarettes. 'It's just not done any more. We're definitely not that far along with Airbnb that it's not the done thing, but I do see it in discussions with friends and hoteliers. You are participating in something which is causing a disturbance,' she said.

Chappell had already taken a moral stand on his use of the platform, triggered by an experience with a host called Brian in LA who just didn't know when to quit, offering a personal service above and beyond that included hand-delivering Amazon parcels. This expanded itself into a refusal to use accommodation that was clearly a home and not an investment, although Chappell felt that, really, the morality of the piece shouldn't be laid at his, or Brian's, door, but with the world's politicians, because, well, it's what we pay them for. He said:

'They have a moral duty to act if Airbnb is driving up rents – then they have to act. If they don't, then I'm operating in the belief that it's OK. The backlash will come on a city-wide level and will probably take the form of what happened in New York when it decided it didn't want Amazon: they are just going to say "thanks, but no thanks" and then it's up to the people who live there to make sure that their elected representatives are stopping that from going on. If there's a town where there's a high supply and high demand, it's fantastic. When it's not, there are problems.'

The moral fibre of guests might not yet be feeling the stress, but protests in Amsterdam, Barcelona, Dubrovnik and many other points along the geographical alphabet had turned against the homesharing platforms. In 2016, residents of New Orleans held a jazz funeral at city hall, with coffins reading 'RIP real neighbours' and 'RIP affordable housing', to protest and mourn neighbourhoods lost to Airbnb tourism. Not the welcome that one was necessarily looking for when one sought to 'live there'.

The customer is always right

While the data on how much homesharing was going on, and exactly where it was happening, was hard to come by, those who were using it were very much the Chatty Cathys. BVA BDRC's Hotel Guest Survey 2016 reported that, in the US, 44 per cent of those staying in a home would otherwise have stayed in a hotel. In the UK, this was 29 per cent; in China, 66 per cent; in Australia, 37 per cent; in Brazil 42, per cent; and in France, 45 per cent[45].

---

[45]www.bva-bdrc.com/opinions/new-facets-home-rental-round-hotel-alternatives-event/

The company did not survey 'amateurs', but talked to people who had also used a branded hotel twice in the previous 12 months. Guests trying Airbnb for the first time cited location and home comforts, with price coming in third. They also wanted to meet other people and indulge in a sense of adventure – although not necessarily at the same time. Business travellers – the customer pool that the hotels most feared being sucked up by Airbnb – commented on the choice of available product, and the chance to be closer to their teams and foster a more collaborative relationship. Guests were also drawn to the opportunity *not* to meet other people in the hotel's breakfast buffet, but instead to be able to choose to sit around drinking their morning coffee unbothered. They were less pleased when they realised they also had to clean up the cup afterwards.

Peers and the pressure they exert was another factor in homesharing's growth. The desire to show off has been with us ever since someone splattered themselves with purple eating a snail and thought 'screw you guys, it's not a spill, it's a fashion statement'. The good news for those of us living within buzzing distance of the Internet was that we had platforms to allow us to broadcast every act of one-upmanship, and the homesharing segment provided the perfect opportunity to feed these platforms. Because what could be more unique than a home?

It was easy to accuse people of living only by reflection, when so many of us were shallow if you were to dig not so far beneath the surface and, in these times when some platforms seemed only to broadcast darkness, what was the harm in a little shallow? Homesharing gave us a valuable chance to look a little more special than we might if we were staying in the local hotel.

The reassuring news for our souls was that homesharing went deeper than that. Consumers had moved from consuming possessions to consuming experiences – although, in many cases, this was because those possessions had become too expensive to consume.

Sheppard, who saw this in the furniture revolution that tossed any number of flower-patterned velour three-piece suites out into the street, said: 'I grew up in the era where Habitat exploded and I thought, "Well, I will buy a modern sofa for my house". It might have taken me 12 instalments to pay for it, but you definitely had a period where mortgages versus salaries were such that you could buy your own home and you could furnish it. I look at my children and possession is less important for them because there are so many things which they don't think they will be able to possess. What is more important is experience.

'My generation grew up with people sending us a brochure in the post if we wanted to book a hotel. I'd use a telephone. My children, unless they want to visit a specific hotel, if they are going to visit a destination, like Venice or Rome, they will only use Airbnb, by choice. Partly because of value, but also because of space and the delight of the unexpected, the uniqueness of what they're experiencing. Everybody talks about experiential lifestyles these days, but they definitely feel that staying in a Hilton in Venice is not as preferable as staying in a glorious apartment just off St Mark's Square.

'Their preference for experiential ways in which to spend their money, rather than building up a series of possessions, will have made a difference. Whether this equalises in the last 10 or 15 years of their working life, I'm not sure yet. But it is very interesting to see almost a harking back to the hippie years, which were all about sharing – free love for everyone. There is a sense that I'm not spending my money to possess, I'm doing this to have had a punctuation mark in my life.'

The sharing economy also appealed to those suffering from the rise of loneliness and disconnection in modern society, many of whom were the early adopters of homestays – the millennials. In *Loneliness: Human Nature and the Need for Social Connection*[46], University of Chicago social

---

[46]https://psycnet.apa.org/record/2008-07755-000

neuroscientist John T. Cacioppo warned that a sense of social isolation could damage both our mental and physical health, as much as obesity or smoking.

Cacioppo said that the pain of loneliness engendered a fear response 'so powerfully disruptive that even now, millions of years later, a persistent sense of rejection or isolation can impair DNA transcription in our immune cells. This disruption also impairs thinking, willpower, and perseverance, as well as our ability to read social signals and exercise social skills. It also limits our ability to internally regulate our emotions—all of which can combine to trap us in self-defeating behaviors that reinforce the very isolation and rejection that we dread. Loneliness shows each of us how to overcome this feedback loop of defensive behaviors to achieve better health and greater happiness.' For society, he said, the potential pay-off was the greater prosperity and social cohesion that follows from increased social trust.

The homesharing platforms – and the clue is in the name here – were eager to make hay with the idea of a home-from-home, somewhere you could belong. They weren't keeping this aspiration a secret. In 2014, Airbnb launched its new logo, naming the symbol Bélo, which it described as 'the universal symbol of belonging'. In case anyone still felt the need to fall back on their marketing PhDs, this was supported with an advertising campaign around 'belong anywhere'. This evolved into 'don't go there, live there'.

As Dessauvagie noted, that wasn't really up to much if you're going somewhere and then being the worst possible neighbour[47]. Not that this was new behaviour for travellers. As every chambermaid would tell you, the tidiest person becomes a feral beast when faced with a hotel room. Hey, who's looking? But with homesharing, it was a whole neighbourhood

---

[47]Now *there* is an untapped travel niche.

having to listen to you and your musical choices, before judging the pile of empty bottles outside the door.

Belief in the vision of the homesharing offering as a way to be part of a new community was greeted with suspicion by many. For Nicholls: 'It is a sanitised version of authenticity'.

The hope of the hotel sector was that homesharing would fall into the same traps that it had – becoming bland and losing what made it special. Bazin told analysts that Airbnb was losing its way, saying: 'It's something you see with these trendy, sexy brands. They work extremely well for four, five, six years, but then they have to actually adapt to a new business model.

'They were rock solid when the soul of the business was all about "You are meeting a local. He will leave you a bottle of wine, you are recommended to go to a restaurant next door, his name is Patrick, he has a great pizza". Now, two-thirds of Airbnb say it's a host room, but there's no host room and there's no host, it's a serviced apartment. No wine, no host. They lost their soul. They were volume-driven but not emotion-driven.'

There was a growing split between the old-school Airbnb and that which had attracted the real estate investors and their multiple sites. In New York, a study by McGill University[48] found that the top 10 per cent of hosts earned 48 per cent of all revenue in 2017, while the bottom 80 per cent of hosts earned just 32 per cent. Bad news for Clarice and her loom, and bad news for those who wanted a visit resplendent with contact with the natives.

Dessauvagie said: 'Over the entire platform – and considering all the platforms – they cannot deliver on "live like a local". If you are staying in a private room or sharing with someone, usually the host is at home. When you book one of those rooms, you interact with the host, you hear

---

[48]www.sharebetter.org/wp-content/uploads/2018/01/High-Cost-Short-Term-Rentals.pdf

their opinion of the city, you see their way of life and you get to experience that local atmosphere. When you rent an entire home, it's quite easy to consider it just as a serviced apartment or a hotel room, and you don't get to experience the local touch, because the majority of Airbnb listings which are being booked are entire homes.'

For Chappell it was worse, Airbnb was that most awful of all things: desperate, as the platform sought to bring people together, but not necessarily in the best way. An enthusiastic user of Airbnb, he nonetheless found its approach to creating pop-up communities alarming, complaining of emails reading: 'There are 20 people staying nearby, do you want to meet up?' No, he did not. 'Are you out of your mind? It's not my NCT group, these are 20 random strangers. We're not all going to have a pool party, this is so, SO desperate. In the same way as when I check into a hotel, the concierge doesn't say, "There's a great gig tonight, I think the lady in room 303 would like you to take her?" NO! Everyone on the fifth floor! In the pool now! It's not Mykonos.'

Away from the party islands, Christoph Hoffmann, CEO at 25hours Hotels[49] had a lonelier vision of the homesharing guest: 'At the end of the day you have to clean up after yourself, you don't have a bar, you don't have a nice restaurant and you don't have the exchange with people, because you're all by yourself'.

Wagner echoed Hoffmann's reality check: 'Airbnb is a bed and key and that's it. They'd like you to believe that you can dive into the experience, that the host can offer you some local colour and knowledge and I suppose that happens occasionally. It is, for the most part, a myth. It's not really a

---

[49]Nine hotels and just the one brand at the start of 2019, AccorHotels acquired a 30 per cent stake in the group in 2017 because, of course. The police were called to a party at its hotel in Berlin during the International Hotel Investment Forum in 2017, earning the venue and wider group a soft spot in the sector's heart. CEO Hoffmann has been inspired by the *Grand Budapest Hotel*, which only serves to seal the deal.

service, it's hard budget accommodation for a type of traveller who cannot afford travel.'

Nicholls had been put off by some of the platform's advertising on public transport, as it sought to pull in that all-important supply by pointing out that extra cash earned by the host could pay for holidays and football season tickets. That, she said: 'Doesn't sound very welcoming. It's become a big brand and you will get a backlash of tourists not getting what they expected to get on Airbnb. It has become a commodity, there's no personal touch'.

Where Airbnb then started to apply effort to hold on to its relationship with the guest was through the experience element, a move it heralded with a presentation that chatted about fairy stories as only a company that had been accused of being a unicorn could. Not just hosts, but anyone with an experience could now offer them on the platform. At Airbnb's Open LA event[50], CEO Brian Chesky said: 'A lightbulb went off – homes are just one part of the journey. This is where we realised we needed to create a holistic travel experience – the whole trip. If you want to have an amazing trip, you end up basically on a research project. You're in line, you're lonely, you're outside, and you're doing things locals never do. We put homes, experiences and places together in one place, to be both magical and easy. These are handcrafted experiences which allow you to immerse yourself in the community, organised by city and by passion. These aren't tours, they are experiences. You immerse.'

This immersion ran the gamut from wine tasting to scavenger hunts via LGBTQ history tours, and in 2018 it was extended to the business sector, to include items such as team-bonding experiences. What's so wrong with just offering a different type of biscuit from that in the office, in a different meeting room, possibly in a windowless hotel basement,

---

[50]*Hotel Analyst*, 14 December 2016

was anyone's guess, but employees could now think about strategy while making jewellery.

There were some who felt this effort to gild the lily is unlikely to produce the required sheen. Bertrand Bazin, CEO and co-founder of Cariboo, which links local guides to visitors around the world, said: 'Airbnb Trips is very good news. They will democratise travel experiences with locals and we are confident that they will not succeed in recruiting the right people to recruit, train and animate those passionate locals. The truth is, you can't diversify so easily. Airbnb has a brilliant skill set in providing local housing solutions but they do not have the culture to offer unique local experiences. And we do!'[51] In 2017 Cariboo started to work with Accor[52] on its experience offering.

Accor was not alone. While Airbnb was looking to get all over the journey and keep the guest for itself, Expedia Group (which owned homestay brand HomeAway) was also adding an 'experience' button for its suppliers, to help properties to create a custom list of cultural landmarks, unique activities and experiences in their local neighbourhoods that could be viewed on their property's listing

Away from making a nice new mug on your weekend away, what Expedia Group and its fellow OTAs noted was that one of the main experiences people wanted was convenience. Really, appallingly so. De Jong was willing to be appalled himself at how much he, well, valued his own time, preferably untainted by being mucked around. He said: 'I'm guilty myself, I book on Booking.com because it's so fricking simple.' Call Booking's marketing department, there's a new gun in town. Airbnb had 7 million-plus listings. There was a fair chance that you're going to find something you like, at a price that you like

---

[51] *Hotel Analyst*, 14 December 2016
[52] These Bazins get everywhere.

and at a time when you need. We're all busy, important people, at least in our minds, who should be able to waste time on our own terms, not on finding accommodation. It also offered products such as split payment.

Bland said: 'The challenge [Airbnb] presents is that someone is providing a way for consumers to transact as they would like to. They want to transact online, they want to see what they are getting, they want something different, they want something unique, they want something that's not run of the mill, and they are able to get that pretty cheaply and pretty quickly. They don't want to feel like they're just another number, just part of the system.'

Personal touches or not, what homesharing has appreciated but the hotel sector, with its brand-driven growth, had lost sight of, was that, as Essex said: 'It's not about your product any more, it's about the customer, it's about what Mark wants.'

What Mark wanted would fuel the success of the hospitality sector's response to homesharing. Because, as we have learned in the evolving role of the consumer, what Mark wants, Mark gets.

The host with the most – in which Airbnb made hoteliers of us all

For Clarice and her loom, homesharing had, as Dessauvagie said, made 'everyone who is a host on Airbnb part of the hospitality industry'.

De Jong was able to comment from the coalface, where hospitality had shown itself to run in the family. He said: 'My sister is renting out her flat in Amsterdam and you get AppleTV with it, you can open the door with your mobile, she has a Chromecast, so, by herself she's already being a better hotelier than most hoteliers. That's where the storm meets – between distribution, giving it a bit of sell, but at the same time it's disrupting the whole industry and also the consumer who comes in through the door and expects a lot from you. For a lot of traditional hoteliers it's hard to keep up with. It has become a word, "I'm going to Airbnb my apartment", even if you put it on Booking you're still Airbnbing your apartment. It's additional supply and it doesn't come into the market when rates are low. If I look at my sister, she checks the conferences to see when the doctors are in town and then she books her holidays. That's when she will release her one-room supply into the Amsterdam market.

'It's not that the doctors want to stay in an Airbnb – there might be 10,000 doctors coming into a city than has 40,000 rooms – but it means that there's extra pressure on the market, so the normal people who would not pay €450 to stay in a hotel would be happy to pay €200 to stay in my sister's apartment. They are people who would have to pay in a hotel, all of a sudden [they] have an option.'

While this move into hospitality may not have extended itself to complying with the same legislation and taxation regimes as the hotel sector, it did come with distribution charges to get those rooms on to the market, which could go as high as 25 per cent of revenue on certain platforms.

Aside from the attraction of Airbnb being the market leader, there was a strong financial pull to use it to list. For home rentals, it took a 3 per cent cut of each booking, along with a 6 per cent to 12 per cent service fee from guests, unlike other platforms, where the guest bore none of the cost. This attracted the attention of rivals, with Expedia Group CEO Mark Okerstrom telling the group's Explore18 conference: 'We've got a tonne of respect for Airbnb, they solved a need to get this rental offering online. They've got a great brand and a great reputation. Airbnb is sharing a 3 per cent commission and then charging the customer sometimes uncapped fees; we are looking very closely at how we are pricing our services.'

According to Bank of America Merrill Lynch[53], Airbnb had 48 per cent of its listings in Europe, with another 23 per cent coming from North America as of August 2018. It said: 'While the listings on its website are extremely diverse, Airbnb tends to skew toward major cities where there is a critical mass of both potential room supply and high prevailing hotel room rates that make home-sharing economics more attractive for potential hosts.' Just like de Jong's savvy sister in Amsterdam.

Airbnb itself appreciated how lovely and cheap it was and showed its ankle to the hotel sector, where distribution costs had driven not only pitched tar-feather-and-fire battles with the OTAs, but also changed the make-up of the hotel sector, driving M&A to achieve negotiating scale on commissions. The platform opened itself up to small, independent hotels and B&Bs, with Cameron Houser, Airbnb's programme manager for hotels, commenting: 'We are dedicated to working with small hospitality businesses that excel at offering the best guest experiences and living our mission of belonging.'[54]

Sheppard was one of those helping Airbnb with its mission. He said: 'We have linked Airbnb to six of our hotels and typically about 18 per cent of our bookings come from Booking, about 9 per cent from Expedia and currently about 1.5 per cent through Airbnb. They are fantastic, they are cheaper in terms of commission, they deliver, the speed of response is good, and their system is just as robust as any other OTA's. I'm sure they'll reach a point where they have enough market share to take parity with the other OTAs and all charge the same rapacious sum, but at the moment they are trying to gain market share by charging less. Any hotelier who can distribute his room more cheaply than Booking is very happy.'

---

[53]BAML *Lodging Primer*, 11 September 2018
[54]www.siteminder.com/news/airbnb-global-hotel-technology-partnership-boutique-hotels-bed-breakfasts/

Airbnb may have been delivering a more advantageously priced guest but also, as Simona Thompson, owner of 4 Percy Place, Bath, had found, a different type of guest. She said: 'As a host I see a huge difference in the clients that come to me through Airbnb or, say, Booking. People who come to me through Airbnb are usually well educated and they are interested in the experience, they appreciate it if you welcome them and talk to them, spend time with them. They ask questions before arriving and they ask about recommendations for dinner or drinks, they ask what can we do, what would you recommend, what places would you suggest we visit. They are more inquisitive. Guests from Booking just want the keys, they have different expectations, they expect a B&B to have the same service as a hotel.

'Airbnb clients call or email before to tell you when they're arriving, or warn you if there's a delay – they are much more respectful, they are aware that they are a guest in your house, but at the same time they feel more welcome. They understand that you're doing your best to make them feel welcome. They like the friendliness, they like the fact that they can ask you things, that you are open to their requests and they appreciate the fact that you are sharing your space with them, that you are sharing your house. It's a different attitude. I don't know whether this is because of the Airbnb ethic or the guests. Airbnb clients look for a relationship with their host, Booking ones don't. My favourite guests are the ones who come with Airbnb.'

PART TWO

HOW DID WE GET HERE? THE ROAD FROM HOLIDAY INN TO IN-ROOM BOREDOM

Hotels have long looked like something people might want to make money from. Customer walks in through revolving door. Customer hands over money. Customer spends majority of time unconscious. Customer gets up, eats and leaves, and the product is fully reusable after a quick dust down. Repeat.

But while the concept looked simple enough, the execution kept many investors out of the game. Housekeeping staff, check-in staff, restaurant staff, decorators, spa staff, pool cleaners, sheet ironers, people to fix broken doors, people to wear gold tassels on their shoulders next to the doors, people to tell guests where to shop, people to tell guests the WiFi codes in the meeting rooms, replacing TVs thrown out of the window by rock stars, calling the authorities when guests were crushed by the TVs thrown out of the windows by rock stars, selling the rooms themselves … day after day after day.

Despite all this, the potential of hotels retained a powerful allure. Daily revenue, with the bonus of capital appreciation on top. Cyclical, but with global diversity to take the edge off.

The first signs of a split between owning a hotel but not having to clean up bits of TV came in the 1960s in the US, with the creation of the real estate investment trust (Reit), which gave everyone access to income-producing real estate. It wasn't until the 1990s that hotel Reits caught the eye of investors and the structure was adopted by countries including France, Germany and the UK (the latter had so far failed to produce a hotel Reit of its own, but a valiant effort was made in 2007 with Vector Hospitality).

With investors finally able to put their money in hotels, but keep themselves clean and clear, hotels also started to look into ways to shed their expensive real estate and use it to fund growth. Marriott International was the first to call in the property brokers as it sought to colonise the US in the 1970s. Holiday Inn had set the tone in the 1960s with a move into franchising, which allowed it to expand and brand build with a vehemence that other flag wavers wanted to emulate. Investors, like guests, found reassurance in brands. The hotel operators' shareholders were also benefitting from the returns on asset sales.

Recent years have seen an acceleration in this move away from owning both the bricks *and* the brand. According to Boston Consulting Group (BCG)[1], the move from asset heavy to asset light 'played out dramatically in the hotel sector in the first decade of this century. At that time, hotel chains reduced their asset ownership, selling most of their properties and, in many cases, using the capital released to expand into developing economies, where room demand was projected to grow far faster than in developed markets. For hotels and other companies seeking to shed fixed

---

[1]www.bcg.com/en-gb/publications/2014/business-model-innovation-growth-asset-light-is-right.aspx

assets such as real estate, a simple sell-and-lease-back contract does not do the trick: the fixed rent is considered a long-term liability. A better option is to negotiate a variable rent, which is typically based on a percentage of earnings, revenues, or some other predetermined factor.'

BCG pointed to Accor, which from 2005 through 2010 sold €4 billion in properties, paying rent that was based on a percentage of hotel revenues. Using a franchise model or a long-term management contract in which the local hotel owner paid a branded hotel chain to manage the hotel also got assets off the balance sheet, with picking between the two structures the favoured choice for most operators.

The consultancy said that, by 2014, the five largest hotel chains' ownership of assets was around one-third lower per revenue dollar than it had been in 2002. 'Executives face a tough dilemma when considering asset weight,' said BCG. Getting shot of the family silver was soon gaining the popular vote.

Not for all. At Accor, the company's asset-right-not-asset-light policy was an outlier, with the group still owning or leasing around 40 per cent of its hotels in 2012, although at that point it had a stated goal of cutting this back to 20 per cent. Still quite the lump on the balance sheet, at a time when Marriott International and InterContinental Hotels Group only held around 1 per cent of their hotels.[2]

There were some for whom the goal wasn't being met fast enough, largely Sébastien Bazin, the then-European head of Colony Capital, the largest shareholder of Accor. Bazin had been needling for a speedier sell-off since 2005 and, in 2013, replaced chairman and CEO Denis Hennequin, who, despite his background at McDonald's, was not felt to be providing the fast fill that investors wanted when it came to the group's global portfolio.

In addition to keeping his foot on the brake, Hennequin resisted pressure to split Accor's property holdings from its hotels business,

[2]http://aparaskevas.blogspot.com/2013/08/accor-group-transformation-to-asset.html

something Bazin got right on to, announcing[3] that by the end of that year the group would split into a HotelServices' division – a management and franchise company – and HotelInvest – a hotel owner and investor. All 1,400 hotels owned by HotelInvest would be operated by HotelServices through management contracts. These would form part of HotelServices' total portfolio of nearly 3,600 hotels.

'Accor is a strong and unique group poised to derive benefit from rich opportunities. However, it deserves a much higher ambition to create sustained value. It requires the in-depth, rapid transformation of its business model and its organisation, as well as a clear and long-term vision, and to stay the course. With this new strategy, our aim is to unlock Accor's full potential through its two core activities and maximise value creation for shareholders,' said Bazin.

The new strategy was designed to give the company a 'value-oriented, disciplined hotel ownership strategy', ending its reliance on expansion through leases. It also said that no more owned hotels would be sold, 'unless they are structurally underperforming assets'.

In 2018[4], Accor sold 57.8 per cent of the assets in AccorInvest, releasing €4.6 billion in cash, with the holdings split between PIF, GIC, Colony NorthStar, Crédit Agricole Assurances and Amundi, and other private investors. The properties would remain as Accor-branded hotels, under long-term agreements. Accor said that it would sell its remaining stake down to 30 per cent, at which point a five-year lockdown would be put in place. After that point, the stake would be cut further[5]. The group had finally gone asset light.

---

[3]www.investegate.co.uk/ArticlePrint.aspx?id=20131127082701P0009
[4]https://press.accorhotels.group/accorhotels-initiates-sale-of-majority-stake-in-accorinvest/
[5]Accor promptly announced that it was considering a move on Air France-KLM, but sadly for fans of world domination, it decided against it. After all, the previous year had seen it acquire a 50 per cent stake in Orient Express from SNCF. Let the train take the strain.

For those who retained ownership but were looking for another exit, the Reit structure remained interesting. In 2018, Hilton was one of the last of the groups to take the option, making good on a three-way split, which it announced in 2016, and saw it spin off the timeshare business as well as moving 70 of its owned hotels into a Reit.

Chris Nassetta, the company's president and CEO, told analysts: 'Each segment should benefit from a dedicated management team with the capital and resources available to take advantage of both organic and inorganic growth opportunities. We believe it will also allow investors to more effectively allocate capital towards businesses more in line with their objectives.' Nassetta said that the companies would look to a variety of growth strategies, commenting: 'If that includes inorganic opportunities, then they certainly will have the capability to pursue those'. He added: 'These businesses ... are going to be set up to be the leaders in each of their segments and to be able to do everything that they need to do to be successful and grow long-term value.'

Nassetta said that the Reit would 'probably' be the second-largest lodging Reit and one of the most geographically diverse, with 'a high-quality portfolio of luxury and upper upscale hotels located across high barrier-to-entry urban and convention markets, top resort destinations, select international markets, and strategic airport locations'. It would be made up of predominantly US-based hotels, which, the CEO said, would 'be appealing to the Reit investor base'.

The Reit would have 'very long tenure agreements' with the operating company. Looking at the OpCo, Nassetta said that the existing fee base had 'tremendous upside potential', which would combine with new unit growth, the latter of which he described as 'easy'.

Nassetta, who had experience with lodging Reits from his time as president and CEO at Host Hotels & Resorts, the Reit spun out of Marriott Corporation in 1993, concluded: 'Through capital allocation at the right

times in the right ways, [we] can create a significant amount of value.
I would hope that ultimately the markets will decide that there will be a
great level of receptivity to a company that will be a very large cap.'

The move was welcomed by JPMorgan Chase & Co, which said in a
note that it made 'sense by simplifying the businesses and should result in
a higher net-valuation multiple'.

The Reit, which was named Park Hotels & Resorts, was quick to cut its
holdings outside the US, having an ownership interest in just four hotels
outside of the country by the start of 2018, accounting for approximately
1 per cent of the EBITDA (earings before interest, tax, depreciation and
amortisation), down from 14 hotels and 5 per cent respectively held at
the beginning of the year. In addition to pulling back to its domestic
market, the group also announced plans to shop outside its own sphere for
operators. Tom Baltimore, Park's chairman and CEO, told analysts on the
group's Q1 2018 earnings call: 'We could use the opportunity to diversify
both brand and by operator. And we certainly like the families of brands –
both Marriott and Hyatt come to mind, among others. We want to grow
and expand our relationships.'

There was, of course, still some nuance to be had from the other global
branded operators when it came to ownership. Marriott International
refused to go so asset light that it floated off entirely and continued to
fund strategic hotels – those that were launching brands or where it
absolutely had to be located and there was no better way to mark its
territory. One example of this was the launch of the Edition brand,
where the group had formed a joint venture with Ian Schrager[6] in 2008
to create a competitor to W[7] and a new offering in the luxury lifestyle

---

[6] And don't think that the design community didn't freak out at the idea of their god working with
Marriott International, either.

[7] Which Marriott International then acquired as part of the Starwood Hotels & Resorts takeover,
but never mind: SCALE IS ALL. And as Schrager told *The Economist* in 2013: 'Everybody used
to think that only people who wore black and lived in Soho came to my hotels. They didn't get
how big the market was.'

market. Not a venture to muck up, Marriott International bought the Berners hotel in London to give the brand the jump it needed in Europe, selling the hotel to the Abu Dhabi Investment Authority in 2014, one year after it had opened.

Being forced deeper into ownership for competitive reasons also saw Radisson Hospitality[8] take a fresh look at leases, announcing plans to take on up to €400 million of lease risk as it looked to expand in Europe. The group said that the decision was taken in part because of the increased demand for leases from institutional investors targeting the hotel sector, as it came closer to being viewed as a mainstream option.

Knut Kleiven, deputy president and CFO at Radisson Hospitality, said: 'There will be some new leased hotels over the next few years but the difference is that that they will be in strong locations. In the UK, this would be locations like London, Manchester, Edinburgh and Glasgow, but not places like Thurrock and West Bromwich. Our development strategy will not change in the emerging markets, where we have 90 per cent of our pipeline. Of course, there is more competition for hotels in primary locations such as Paris and Rome, and we don't feel that we are any different to any other hotel company. In Western Europe, everyone needs to put some money in your offer, whether that is through performance guarantees or leases; there is a need for some kind of commitment.'[9]

One other area where the branded companies found themselves forced to use charming terms such as 'skin in the game' was Africa, which had been lingering around giving off great wafts of potential for a number of

---

[8]Formerly Rezidor, the company was last seen being majority owned by Jin Jiang International Holdings, which bought a stake off fellow China-based investor HNA Group, with reports suggesting that their government had objected to HNA's rather high-profile spending spree and ordered it to sell up. The co-founder of HNA then slipped off a cliff in the south of France. We take the 'then' under advisement, because accidents happen, but it sure did freak everyone out at the time. Radisson Hospitality was run alongside Radisson Hotel Group of which Jin Jiang International Holdings owned 100 per cent, having bought that from HNA. Brands included Radisson, Park Inn and other flags featuring the word 'Radisson'.
[9]*Hotel Analyst*, August 2018

years, but where very few had managed to make inroads[10] other than, not-that-oddly, Radisson Hospitality, which, under its former moniker of Rezidor, had launched a fund, Afrinord, alongside several Nordic development funds. This fund was created in 2014, building on a joint venture set up in 2005, and provided equity financing to hotel owners and developers in Africa.

Wolfgang Neumann, then-CEO and president of Rezidor, said at the time: 'We have adjusted our business model to the current market conditions across Africa. We respond to today's needs and offer a unique combination of management services, technical assistance and sliver equity. Afrinord underlines our firm commitment to the powerful emerging market of Africa. It enables us to drive selected hotel developments and to help our regional owners and business partners to reach project completion in time and on budget.'[11]

Around a decade after Rezidor was gaining traction in Africa by putting money where its mouth was, Hilton Worldwide and Accor both announced funds to push growth in the region. The former's, featuring $50 million, was to be spread over 100 hotels, while the latter's, for $1 billion – with the help of Katara Hospitality – had no specific targets other than 'to accelerate our dynamic growth trajectory in the Sub-Saharan region'.

Just throwing money at the continent was unlikely to be enough – Hilton Worldwide was also working on new methods of construction in the region. Trevor Ward, owner of the W Hospitality Group, said of Accor's fund: 'This is a terrific announcement and a game changer if they can spend it, which I don't think is going to be that easy [as] they are going

---

[10]Marriott International made a strong showing with the purchase of Protea Hospitality in 2014, but the fact of those underdeveloped regions was that, well, there's nothing there to buy yet, so just flinging cash around wasn't going to help.
[11]www.rezidor.com/static-files/ed67bc2f-0abd-4afe-9315-150f20316e57

to take a while to spend it. This is for acquisitions and greenfield and they will have to be opportunistic. There are hotels to buy, but we suffer from over-priced assets and people have a very inflated sense of value. For the greenfield, it will be around product delivery, how to get it done, finding the team that can deliver.'

But in the main, the hotel sector was unwilling to pile into ownership in any significant fashion. Having leapt off the property ladder, it was now a happy renter.

While the hotel operators were busy selling off their assets, the world was making its transition towards all things branded, as the name of your sweatshirt moved from the label in the neck to being emblazoned across the front. Similarly, hotels no longer saw their future in terms of real estate curation, but in creating and expanding brands.

Growth through fees became the thing, with hotels freed from all sorts of horrid fixed costs in the process. Let the owners worry about those. This, one might – or might not – be surprised to learn, in the otherwise hospitable world of hospitality, led to some animosity between the brands and the owners, with many feeling that the risk was now all piled on to the owner, while the reward was heaped on the brand. The latter of which was not making any friends by doing things like demanding the mattresses were changed to their bespoke offering with every brand refresh.

Emboldening owners was a tentative move away from brands by that other interested party – the lenders. Bob Silk, relationship director at Barclays Bank, told the 2016 International Hotel Investment Forum in Berlin that a flag was no longer a prerequisite for a loan, commenting: 'The key word for us is cashflow. As the world came to an end in 2007, the lending community became obsessed with LTV, which is flawed. Our focus is on cash and making sure that we don't lend past what the borrower can afford. There was a flight towards cash after the crash and now we're coming out the other end of that, and a lot of the competition we're seeing is LTV lenders. So the circle has turned and it will again.' If you could get cash into the tills, the banks no longer sought comfort in the flag over the door.

Desmond Taljaard, managing director, hotels at London & Regional Properties, told delegates: 'Five or 10 years ago, lenders would often appear to collude with the management company to have a non-disturbance agreement put in to protect the value of the asset. Brands used to be a lucky rabbit's foot that you would cling to. There has been a sea change.'

At the same event one year later, Taljaard had warmed to his theme[12]: 'What would a brand have to be able to do to put a brand on a hotel? They need to drive business above and beyond what the hotel could do itself. The economics are going to come under lots of scrutiny when the contracts come up for renewal. Every time a brand hires a new brand leader, it adds new costs for me: they add bacon at breakfast, green carpet, blue carpet. It's wonderful for that person's CV and I hope they do well, but it adds cost for me. Brands need to keep the cost of value added in balance.'

Speaking on the Forum sidelines, Robert Shepherd, chief development officer, Europe at IHG, had a defence: 'The old days of a 25- or 30-year management agreement that you couldn't get out of, they're gone. The point now is around aligning interests. Unless we align interests, there is no point in a 20-year relationship. By structuring – whether there are performance tests, whether there is a hurdle for incentive management, so you don't earn meaningfully until you get a certain level of GOP. Our fee structures are a base and an incentive fee, the base is low and competitive. We will talk to owners at the outset and start to make an agreement based on their interests.

'We don't have to have capital in the game; we don't have to own it, but we can make sure that our performance is tied to the hotel performance.

---

[12] As anyone who has spent any time in the Marlene Bar in Berlin will tell you, not an unusual state for Desmond.

There may be guarantees for the first five or six years, at which point the owner will refinance a stabilised asset.[13]'

The branded operators needed to make a convincing case for why their layer of cost was needed at all, as the great wave of franchising spread out from the US. As hotel brands moved away from both ownership and operations, the onus was on them to prove why they were worth a damn, particularly as the OTAs were selling their wares not only in terms of a route to market, but, increasingly, operations-related services. One OTA, Ctrip, even launched its own brand: Rezen Hotel Group[14].

The touch of the brands was getting lighter and lighter and further away from their historic roots as asset owners. A survey undertaken by BLP in 2016 backed the trend towards franchising, reporting that it was expected to be the most important source of growth for the global operators. The report said: 'Franchising used to be viewed as posing a threat to brand standards, with the flag owner having a much lighter touch than through a more-rigorous management agreement or lease. Now the growth of third-party management companies has provided an added layer of expertise on behalf of the owner and seen standards secured.' As we will see later, it was these third-party operators that gave owners a chance to take the power back.

A brand by any other name would fill the street

So the hotel sector had discovered the power of branding, and neon sign manufacturers around the world rejoiced. So too, initially, did the consumer. By 2019, the number of brands was increasing at the same rate as the national debt clock in Manhattan. Marriott International had 30 just

---

[13]*Hotel Analyst*, 14 March 2017
[14]www.phocuswire.com/Ctrip-ventures-into-hotel-management-with-Rezen-Hotels-Group

to itself and aspirations for more. There were brand families – Mummy and Daddy Holiday Inn, and the kids: Holiday Inn Express, Holiday Inn Club Vacations and Holiday Inn Resort. These weren't new-fangled micro-families – this was the full 'it takes a village'.

Frits van Paasschen, author, citizenM advisory board member, and former Starwood Hotels & Resorts president and CEO, said: 'There was a time when predictability and reliability was what you were looking for in a brand and that certainly applies with hotels. The fact that a five-star hotel was really boring didn't bother me that greatly as I was going somewhere I hadn't been so much and I wanted to make sure I had a clean room that was going to be quiet.'

This need for safety and reassurance became a factor every time the consumer left the house. Kate Nicholls, CEO at UKHospitality, said: 'There was a rush in the 1990s for those big, anonymous hotels. It was the same on the high street. You were attracting a new set of consumers who'd never really eaten out before – this would be the 1980s and 1990s – a new upper working class and lower middle class that wasn't comfortable and they found the reassurance of the brands helpful and the anonymity helpful. They weren't going to get found out using the wrong knife or fork. There was a new affluence in Thatcher's Britain. That's why Beefeater, when it first started, were all little booths, so nobody could see you eat, so you felt comfortable. You had this rush towards the brand, with no nasty surprises – it was still the time where if you went to an independent you might get a horror story, whether that's F&B or a hotel.

'Then you naturally get a backlash against brands. Again, you had the same thing on the high street, you start having anonymous high streets where you could be anywhere in the country and it's the same with some of those hotel brands. They've become victims of their own success. And then they have to reinvent themselves a bit more to show that there's a personal touch.'

Nicholls was not the only observer to see the growth of brands as not quite an unmitigated success. James Woudhuysen, visiting professor, London South Bank University and futurologist, said: 'Hotels need innovating. Retail is retail and very poor on detail. When you go to a hotel you immediately notice that three things are wrong and if it stops there then it's alright. When it gets to four, five, six things then I call management. Why is that? Because there's a productivity crisis in hotels, they are not very good on IT, they are not very good on building management systems, they are not using robots and cleaners and sensors. M&A, private equity and god knows what else have increased the distance between the owners and the franchisees and the customer, and the circuit of branding has increased the cognitive confusion of the customer. The upshot of this is why should anybody care very much? You've got the diffusion of responsibility, where it's always somebody else. If your wastepaper bin isn't empty or the lift is making a noise, in a more diffused structure of ownership and relentless cost cutting, and with the gig economy and immigration as a substitute for genuine capital investment – faster lifts, safer lifts – you've got this general economic rundown which is also true of retail. The robots are not coming.'

For James Bland, director at BVA BDRC, the consumer should share at least part of the responsibility for the cookie-cutter brand approach. He said: 'We are cognitive misers. We will take any mental shortcut that we can. If we have a decision to make, we can look painstakingly at the bedding options for four or five hotels or we can think "Oh, Premier Inn, good night's sleep, Lenny Henry says so", and our brains will always follow the path of least resistance and a brand does that. The brand is the promise, the brand is the representation of the service and product that you respect.'

Bland did not share the opinion of many; that more is less. He said: 'One of the reasons why we have so many hotel brands is that we are much more comfortable as a population with the idea that people have different wants and different needs and different preferences. So the market can support 130 brands, whereas perhaps 20, 25 years ago, 40 was sufficient because we accepted that it wasn't possible to deliver our very specific requirements. Now we don't accept that. We don't think "I will have to change to accept this"; we look for the thing which matches exactly what we want to do and by and large we can order it instantly, pay for it instantly and for the most part it's secure. That is in part what's driving the brands. I don't think that any category is going to disappear, you can see that the rate of growth for a particular brand slows, a few of them will start to flip over, and move into a soft brand. You have to have more brands to drive growth.'

As of 2018, Kit Kat had 200 variants[15], illustrating that customers have, indeed, developed certain specialised tastes and that some of those were Hokkaido Melon with Mascarpone Cheese. However important you thought a Kit Kat was, scale that up to how important your home-from-home was and you have some idea, as Bland noted, of how many brands there were potential for.

Just in case anyone at this point was swelling with the warmth of fulfilled goals and human satisfaction met, the growth of the brands has not all been about providing the consumer with a flag that specialised solely in offering a warm cookie from a special drawer at reception[16]. More brands were needed, in part because every branded contract came with areas of protection to ensure that signing up to a 25-year management contract under one brand need not be followed by the sudden shock of a hotel under the same brand popping up on the corner five years later and making off with your guests.

---

[15]www.thesun.co.uk/fabulous/food/6064324/japanese-japan-kit-kat-flavour-green-tea-soy-sauce-chocolate-bar/

[16]Doubletree by Hilton. The cookie is the key point of differentiation for a brand with very flexible standards. But it is a great cookie.

The operators didn't want sad owners, they wanted more and more growth. To do that they needed more brands to protect themselves from these areas of protection. This ruse had not gone unnoticed by owners and every M&A deal came with a level of attrition as investors found that their hotels were now part of a larger whole – a whole that might include their former competitors – and consequently left the group in order to try their luck elsewhere. Try digging those dropouts out of an annual report.

In 2015, Accor tried another route and opened up its distribution platform, AccorHotels.com, to a selection of independent hotels, with the aim of providing a broader choice of selected hotels to its customers and an alternative booking platform for independent hotels.

The Marketplace initiative was first revealed to *Hotel Analyst* in March 2015, with then-deputy CEO Vivek Badrinath telling the publication: 'Are we open to distributing third-party hotels? Why not? It's an easy yes – in places where we're not. If we want a hotel in Kazakhstan, where we don't have any hotels and it could be added and customers could earn points with the loyalty system. Even in places where they're not in the same catchment area. In Berlin, where we have 25 properties, would we support another 10? Probably. Could we? Why not? Amazon has Marketplace, which is essentially giving their distribution to direct competitors, and they make money out of it.'

The company charged independent hotels a commission of 14 per cent to use the marketplace, with a target of 10,000 within two-and-a-half years. Joining the loyalty scheme was optional, with Romain Roulleau, Accor's then-SVP e-Commerce and digital services, commenting: 'Hotels can opt into the loyalty programme and pay a 5 per cent extra cost, which will enable their guests to earn points on their stay. It allows them to access very regular travellers.'

The company shuttered the project in 2017, however, citing results that were 'below expectations'. The Marketplace initiative had owners grinding their jaws from the get-go, with talk of a number of letters flitting between lawyers' offices from owners wondering why they had bought into a brand and hoisted a flag when any hotel could pay to play. The goals of the operator and the goals of the owners had slid apart at this point and the plan didn't garner enough traction for Accor to make the argument that more scale was better for everyone. Never mind, the company continued launching brands and buying stuff, so spirits were suitably buoyed.

The largest deal in recent years was the $13.6 billion takeover of Starwood Hotels & Resorts[17] by Marriott International, creating a company of more than 5,700 properties and 1.1 million rooms, representing 30 leading brands, from the moderate-tier to luxury, in over 110 countries. With the completion of the acquisition, Marriott International's distribution more than doubled in Asia and the Middle East and Africa combined.

President and CEO Arne Sorenson told the media on a call following the closing of the deal: 'We believe that Marriott now has the world's best portfolio of hotel brands, the most comprehensive global footprint, and the most extensive loyalty programmes, providing an unparalleled guest experience. Combining Starwood's brands with ours better enables Marriott to reach our goal of having the right brand in the right place to serve our loyal guests and welcome new ones. No matter where a customer goes, we've got a place for them to stay. No matter what their budget, we've got a place for them to stay. No matter what the occasion, we've got a place for them to stay.'

---

[17]The company that brought you 11 brands, including Sheraton and W, the latter a hip brand that this correspondent was told by one of the development team was not a brand for actual hip people, but one for the aspiring hip. What the hell, I'll take it. The stable also included the Le Méridien brand, which had been heavily fought over in the past for reasons many remain confused over. It was the scene of a nasty writedown and then exit for financier Guy Hands after he paid £1.9 billion for the company in 2001, a deal that marked the entrance of Hands into a sector largely unaware of his fame as the chief of Terra Firma, leading one CEO of a large US hotel group to whisper 'who is this Gee Hands?' rather loudly during a speech by Hands at the Berlin hotel conference the year after. The company's former CEO, Juergen Bartels, vanished shortly after the transaction, spawning the ever-popular Marlene Bar game: 'Whatever happened to JB?' Answers on a postcard, a prize will be considered.

The transaction marked a shift in thinking, from viewing a hotel company as a collection of brands to a portfolio, an all-you-can-eat buffet for owners who could now park all their hotels, from budget to luxury, with the same group, creating an ecosystem within which Marriott International hoped to collect both investors and customers, all of whom could now join a loyalty company that covered everything from business trips to family holidays.

In its *Hotel Britain* report, BDO had a note of caution for operators looking for growth, commenting: 'As brands race to grow their market share, we have seen significant activity leading to brand acquisition on the premise that this allows increased loyalty, and creates scale and customer touchpoints, as well as potential earnings and driving greater negotiating power with OTAs. But we advise some caution with this approach; the days of growing the number of brands in a stable are over and hotel owners should consider how many brands they can sustainably and profitably maintain.'

As if to underline the point that Sorenson was making – that you market the whole, not the individual parts – Bland said: 'On the demand side, greater individualisation, rejection of "same old, same old" and demand for unique experiences continues to support the case for more brands. Analysts may want fewer brands because it might make their lives a bit easier, but nobody really expects consumers to be aware of every brand out there – nor should that be the aspiration for all but the few genuine behemoths – so it's now as much about portfolio penetration as anything else. That's why we see "by Hilton" and "an IHG Hotel" becoming more common, and advertising campaigns that cover portfolios rather than single brands – Accor's fantastic "from the heart" advert is a prime example.

'On the supply side, the need to circumnavigate non-competitive regions, broaden the reach of the overall system and protect the, now mostly intangible, balance sheet by spreading risk hasn't gone away. It would also require a fairly large about-turn for the big brand houses to now change their minds and claim that, actually, they have too many brands. Given how much has been said, publicly, about adding – or, in the case of Marriott, maintaining – brands, it's the sort of U-turn that could potentially undermine investors' confidence in leadership and strategy.'

When asked whether Marriott International would consider adding to, or taking away from, its portfolio, Sorenson said: 'The other thing that's important to recognise here is that the biggest expense from a brand perspective is about marketing the brands. And that's most expensive when each brand has to be marketed on its own. The principal model today is to market through our loyalty platform, through our dot-com site, or through our app. And those things allow us to market a portfolio and offer an incredible range of choice to our customers, which drives conversion from looking to booking that much higher and makes the economics of each brand better, not weaker. We're going to keep these brands and we're going to continue to grow them. I don't really think that there are material incremental costs to having a brand, given that that's the business model that we have.'

The takeover did not change Marriott International's thoughts about being asset light, announcing that it was confident that it could sell Starwood Hotels & Resorts' remaining assets for more than $1.5 billion.

Not everyone drank the Kool Aid[18] when it came to the bigger, stronger, faster-than-before Marriott International. Scott Antel, partner, BLP, said: 'There's no doubt that there's going to be an impact on rates. Even if they

---

[18]And neither did Marriott International in 2018, when it discovered a massive data breach. Marriott International, an exemplar in all that is technological, found itself vulnerable after buying Starwood Hotels & Resorts, which was less, well, exemplary. *Caveat emptor.*

didn't price fix, the market share means it's inevitably going to happen. Maybe that's good for the owner, shared services and the like, but do you want to be entirely in bed with one operator? I don't think it's doing anyone a favour in terms of scale, it's for the shareholders.

'They're pitching this as wonderful for owners as it gives economies of scale and push-back against the OTAs. If you're running a hotel that's a big box with a lot of little boxes in it, there is probably some merit to that, but when you go up to the higher end and what luxury is all about, which is hospitality, how can you do that when you're a behemoth? When you get so big that there comes a McDonaldisation of scale and you lose that personal touch. They put in brand standards and behavioural standards and you inevitably get automatons. The group has so many brands in the same sectors. Are they going to support the cost of maintaining all these brands or weed a few out? If it's Marriott v. Sheraton, they are going to favour the one with the family name. You could be stuck in a 20-year contract with a flagging brand. I think this is a material change of circumstances, but this brand has a 20-year contract and whatever happens – terrorist attack, influx of disease – the owner has to behave as if nothing has changed. Just because you pass the competition rules doesn't mean it's competitive.'[19]

With the integration of the two companies still chugging along in 2018, two US-based Reits – Pebblebrook Hotel Trust and Diamondrock Hospitality – both complained that the integration was hitting RevPAR, with sales teams suffering. Marriott responded that issues were appearing to be hotel or market specific rather than illustrating trends and that it was seeking to address them.

Host Hotels & Resorts' CFO Michael Bluhm bucked the trend, lending a hand and telling analysts in August of the same year that it had not seen any measurable impact from the sales integration. 'In fact,' he said,

---

'the RevPAR index for our legacy Starwood portfolio actually outpaced that of our Marriott legacy portfolio in the quarter. Furthermore, we continued to reap the benefits from the Marriott Starwood revenue and cost synergies. In particular, we continue to accrue benefits from reduced OTA charges, procurement, credit card, reward and centralised system cost. We're still expecting now a fair amount of expectation around revenue synergies driven by the sales force integration, loyalty programme integration among others. We will continue to monitor and work with Marriott to ensure a smooth transition, and we are very pleased with what we have seen to date'.

Jun Risoleo, Host Hotels & Resorts' CEO, added: 'Whether it's reduced OTA commissions, we'll start seeing a benefit when the rewards programmes are merged, together with lower charge-out ratios on the expense side as we get our Starwood legacy hotels fully integrated into Avendra[20]. We'll see lower procurement costs. We're seeing lower workers' comp costs on Marriott legacy properties as a result of Marriott implementing Starwood workers' compensation policies'.

It was the growth of these brands that was both the offence and defence when it came to the homesharing sector. Blogging[21] about the deal, Sorenson said: 'The hospitality industry today is filled with new and emerging options. Long gone are the days when a Marriott hotel competed against the Hilton hotel across the street. Product quality, great service and brands are still important aspects of our competitive landscape. In recent years, however, we have seen this landscape become more and more complex. With greater sophistication and greater access to information, travellers now have unlimited options, from luxury to

---

[20]Procurement company founded by Marriott International and sold to Aramark in 2013. You think Costco is where the cheap toilet roll is at, you are dangerously naïve. Marriott International's payout on the deal was 4,900 per cent its initial investment. That's some fully quilted luxury if ever I saw it.

[21]And you may well laugh, but Sorenson's predecessor, Bill Marriott Jr, was one of the first CEOs to blog – and to say interesting and relevant things while he was at it.

economy hotels, from traditional to lifestyle, and from well-defined to totally unpredictable.

'Even as the hotel industry itself has become more varied, the methods for planning and booking travel have also become varied – think not just TripAdvisor and Expedia, but Google and Alibaba, which all provide services and seek to make a profit in our industry. Then, add home-sharing platforms like Vrbo, Home Away and Airbnb. While each is very different from the other, they look a bit like a combination of an intermediary and a traditional competitor. So what do we do? First, we want to expand our offerings to ensure we have the right product in the right place to serve our loyal guests and capture new ones. Second, we want to be big enough to be able to cost-effectively invest in marketing and technology to stay front and centre for our guests. Third, we want to have the best loyalty programmes in the business. This merger does all that.'[22]

And does that it did. And more later about whether loyalty meant loyalty to brand, loyalty for discounts or 'just too dazed at check-in after 16 hours wondering why your doctor-prescribed sleeping medication only worked after the plane had landed' not to join the loyalty programme. For now, the split between bricks and brains had led to the formation of ever-expanding brand stables in much the same way as the Big Bang flung matter into the corners of infinity. As we saw earlier, what came crawling out of the ooze was not for everyone.

As some operators reached 30 brands or more, there were those who stuck with ownership and with just the one flag, simplicity being no bad thing. Lennert de Jong, commercial director at citizenM, pointed to a reaction to the brand behemoths, commenting: 'citizenM was started because of a certain type of traveller. We started for the same reason Airbnb started – we thought "we can do better". We looked at all those

---

[22]www.linkedin.com/pulse/marriott-starwood-merger-growth-choices-value-arne-sorenson/?trk=mp-reader-card

boring experiences that the brands are delivering at the moment. They don't own, they don't manage, they have a ton of flags, and from the inside the rooms are boring and the lobbies are uninspiring. If you travel for business and you stay at a normal Hilton, if you wake up early in the morning the whole lobby is closed and you can't get a cup of coffee, there's no one there who wants to talk to you, you don't have an environment you want to spend time in, you're there in your 27sqm hotel room for the next four hours with a horrible coffee machine and any Airbnb can do better.

'With citizenM we create communal areas. The moment you wake up in the morning you want to get out of bed and get a double espresso to wake you up because it's 5am there but 11am in the country you came from, then there are people sitting in the space and you can get a double espresso because it's open 24/7. When we started citizenM we looked at the frustrations of the business travellers. I think Airbnb is providing a good alternative for people who are going to be on their own anyway early in the morning. Hotels are at least providing decent bars at night, but with the full 24-hour spectrum, the plain vanilla 3 to 4 star hotel can easily be replaced by Airbnb.

'Where do you position citizenM? We're a real estate company that owns our real estate, we operate the hotels ourselves and we manage our own brand. If you don't own your real estate as a brand, how can you control that which distinguishes it? How can you control what an owner will do, that they will buy cheap furniture? Other people think differently, but for us an ownership strategy is key. If you don't own, then you're having to talk to owners about things that you want to do, which makes it hard to execute in fast-moving growth. Look at Autograph, look at Tribute – they are all independent hotels. They pay the big brands for their distribution.'

And right there, de Jong has a point. Back when Accor was experimenting with Marketplace and owners were getting all Jane Austen and whipping out their quills, there was the parallel march towards the soft brands, which very quickly became the hip new thing for every global operator to have. You simply weren't anyone unless you had a brand that looked like it wasn't one of your brands, and if that sounds like a contradiction in terms, then that would be to ignore the evolution that hotel brands have undergone.

It was a persuasive argument. In 2019, citizenM was the latest in a number of hotel companies to attract investors from Asia, when Singapore's sovereign wealth fund GIC acquired a 25 per cent stake in the company, valuing the group at €2 billion.

Branded hotel companies were no longer just providers of a neon sign and a bespoke scent[23], they were a route to market for hotel owners. How you sold your hotel rooms was a battleground where hotels were leaving entrails all over the field. Really disgusting stuff, complete with the live vivisection of profits, as distribution costs devoured the delicious protein, leaving a twitching carcass just about capable of dilating a fearful eyeball. We get into all of this later, if you can stomach it.

Lots of independent hotels weren't interested in being told how to smell by some corporation halfway around the world, but they were certainly interested in accessing their distribution networks and so the soft brand became more and more popular. Such flags meant that a hotel could keep its original name, carpets and thoughts on gin, but by joining Marriott International's Autograph Collection or, indeed, Marriott International's Tribute Portfolio[24], you could access a global sales force, albeit for a fee.

---

[23]Holiday Inn relaunched in 2007. Samples for scents for both Holiday Inn and Holiday Inn Express washed up on sector hacks' desks around the world, leading, one suspects, to several changes of departments, if not addresses. Very citrussy.
[24]Marriott are not kidding with the whole 'scale' bit, you know. There's a third: The Luxury Collection.

And that they did. In 2017, the Wyndham Hotel Group took itself to 19 brands with the launch of The Trademark Hotel Collection[25], a soft brand aimed at upper-midscale and above, which it said was designed for independent entrepreneurs who have built 'an iconic hotel and are looking to boost its distinctive legacy with unmatched support'. Lisa Checchio, Wyndham Hotel Group's VP, brand marketing and insights, said: 'A trademark is a symbol of character, an emblem of individuality. Trademark isn't just another brand: it's a rally cry for independent entrepreneurs who aren't afraid to make their own mark. The Trademark Hotel Collection is the next step in our mission to flip the script on existing expectations and champion all hoteliers by offering them an independent choice outside of the current luxury and upscale options available.'

The issue of trademarking – and the likelihood of Trademark creating an infinite number of 'TM' symbols swirling eventually into a black hole through which we would be sucked into another dimension in which all logic was inverted and either all, or nothing, was branded – was, of course, a matter of concern for the community, responsibility for wider society not always being of utmost concern to the branding marketer.

'The explosion of soft brands in the last several years has been focused on luxury and upscale hoteliers – with demand still growing at a rate of nearly 20 per cent – leaving a market void for independent hoteliers in the upper-midscale segment, the largest segment accounting for 18 per cent of rooms in the US,' said Chip Ohlsson, Wyndham Hotel Group's chief development officer. 'Wyndham is the only hotel company positioned to champion upper-midscale-and-above independent hoteliers so they can compete in an ever-changing distribution environment with brand-backed support and guest recognition and loyalty.'

---

[25]www.prnewswire.com/news-releases/its-time-to-trademark-wyndham-makes-its-mark-on-soft-brands-with-the-trademark-hotel-collection-300467908.html

Wyndham's announcement came shortly after Marriott International said that it would be leaning on its collection brands for growth. 'With our three-tier collection strategy that includes The Luxury Collection, Autograph Collection Hotels and Tribute Portfolio brands, independent hoteliers have more options to leverage Marriott's powerful loyalty and distribution channels, whether through a new build or conversion hotel, depending on the location and physical product,' said Tony Capuano, EVP and global CDO, Marriott International. 'We're seeing increased demand for Marriott's collection brands given consumers' desire to stay at properties with unique stories and independent hotel owners realising that Marriott's size and scale can drive significant value to their properties.'[26]

'Size, scale and choice really do matter in the complicated distribution environment that we are in,' noted Stephanie Linnartz, EVP, chief commercial officer, Marriott International. 'Independent hotels are an invaluable part of our portfolio, because they make our loyalty programme more compelling, our sales efforts more effective and our overall hotel portfolio even more attractive to guests.'

Bland wondered whether the world needed another collection brand: 'Probably not. Is there space for another? Without doubt. I think that's the point – they exist not to occupy space, but to boost a system. They're not intended to make lasting impacts on the mass-market, their purpose is to avoid violating competition territory restrictions, appeal to a broader consumer base, flog a few more rooms in a hotel that perhaps finds itself under the radar and – of course – diversify corporate risk should any particular brand turn toxic.

'Brand awareness (which seems to come and go more quickly than ever before) is still the key to the door for the biggest players, but outside of that is not really the main battleground any more; preference (resulting in

---

[26]http://news.marriott.com/2017/06/marriott-international-embarks-global-independent-hotel-expansion-consumers-owners-seek-unique-experiences-powered-marriott/

conversion) is perhaps more important now, plus price premium, and in both cases there is often something to be said for scarcity; especially when serious volume isn't really an option.'

There were, of course, other routes to market, and groups such as Global Hotel Alliance, an alliance – yes – of independent hotel brands, saying: 'It's a potential threat, but we're dealing with brands, not individual hotels. It would be contradictory for them to join another brand, I'm not aware of any of our brands who have talked to the megabrands. They're simply too expensive – it's a similar price to a hard brand to join a soft band. We don't have the distribution they do, but we're infinitely cheaper and the big brands tend to exaggerate the difference that they make with a luxury or upscale asset – it's likely to be only a few points in occupancy. As you get to the very, very high end of the market there's not even that. I also think there's a change in consumer thinking about brands. People are much more interested in small brands or independents.'[27]

Making a mark for, well, if not the little guy, then certainly the one-brand pony, was Premier Inn, which was named the world's strongest hotel brand by Brand Finance in 2018[28]. Not a mean feat when the company's estate was predominantly located in the UK, with Germany nominated as its growth target, but not at that point having reached anything that could be described as scale in the country. The sale of the Costa Coffee business for £3.9 billion by Whitbread in 2018 was expected to give the brand's growth a caffeinated shot in the arm and headline writers were happy to be thrown a bone.

Frothy headlines aside, at the time of Brand Finance's conclusion, Premier Inn's aspirations in Germany were leaning towards the

---

[27]*Hotel Analyst*, 20 November 2018

[28]http://brandfinance.com/press-releases/marriott-closer-to-checking-in-as-most-valuable-hotel-brand/

lesser-spotted, making its achievement as the world's strongest brand somewhat historic. The brand valuation and strategy consultancy said: 'The mass-market, UK-focused brand's top billing may come as a surprise to some, however Premier Inn lives up to its name across a broad range of brand metrics, from marketing investment to familiarity and consideration. Luxury brands may be notionally more desirable, but they are not as widely known as Premier Inn. The budget chain's value for money also supports higher scores for preference and satisfaction. Premier Inn's financial performance is correspondingly strong, with total sales up 12.9 per cent and like-for-like sales up 4.2 per cent in their financial year 2015/16, supporting an 11.9 per cent pre-tax profit increase for Whitbread.

'Whitbread has consistently invested in effective marketing communications. Premier Inn was the first mass-market UK hotel brand to be advertised on prime-time television following its creation in 2007 and has benefitted from high-quality, effective advertising (frequently fronted by the comedian Sir Lenny Henry) ever since. As confidence has grown in the strength of the brand, campaigns have become more emotionally led. Recent ads focus on Premier Inn's role in helping friends and family keep in touch, including the Wes Anderson-inspired "Aunt Mabel's Birthday".'

The company warned that the operating environment for many major hotel brands was becoming increasingly challenging, particularly due to changing customer demands and technology. The advent of Airbnb had, it said, allowed access to a vast range of private accommodation that played into a growing desire for unique, visually interesting and 'authentic' accommodation. Airbnb's brand value was, it said, growing more rapidly than any of the major hotel brands. It increased 52 per cent year-on-year to reach a total of $3.7 billion in 2017, making it more valuable than all but four of the world's biggest hotel brands.

While Premier Inn was hailed as the strongest brand, Hilton, Marriott and Hyatt were named as one, two and three in terms of most valuable. Robert Haigh, marketing and communications director at Brand Finance, said: 'There are advantages to the mono-brand strategy – your revenue is focused. There are also direct cost savings and resources are more concentrated. It's also easier to build brand awareness – every time the brand appears, you are reinforcing it. If you have a house of brands you don't have those same advantages, although having a pool of brands means that, should a scandal hit, you do avoid contagion, although this is not something which tends to affect the hotel sector.'

And just like that, we were back to de Jong, who could smell the writing on the wall for the megabrands and those who would exhale them. He said: 'It's always going to take a generation. Hilton and Marriott have a lot of brand awareness, but it's almost like smoking. A lot of governments have made a smoke-free generation. We're of the same generation that grew up smoking everywhere and it's the same generation that went to Holiday Inn for the consistency. But if you look at future generations, what they do for travel, where they go, what are their criteria for the places they choose to stay? It's not going to be the plain vanilla big brand box – they're not putting on Instagram "I'm staying at the Hilton".

'If you look at Instagram, you can see that something good has come from globalisation: local brands have a chance, and individual entrepreneurs have been given the same chance as big brands. It's the same in music – it went from bundles, to unbundled, to bundled, and with Spotify the power is back to the musicians.'

De Jong's colleague at citizenM, van Paasschen, warned that those segments of the branded market that no one could pick out of a line-up were at risk of being killed off by their own, well, dullness, turning off consumers and investors alike.

He said: 'At citizenM, where we want to create a really fun, high-energy public area, we don't want to spend a lot on F&B because we're in big cities where we know there's lots of alternatives, but we know people want to have an espresso or a drink or a grab'n'go breakfast. They're very comfortable in a small room because all they do there is shower and sleep and maybe watch a movie, but for the rest of the time they want to do everything in a well-designed public area.

'The real estate utilisation of a building like that means that you have twice the number of rooms in a hotel of traditionally the same size, you have a better experience and you have lower operating costs because most of what has been done has either been outsourced or centralised or not fully implemented, such as F&B. It creates a different proposition and that's one where you can have capital flow to and still see growth, whereas those four and five star hotels that were bought 30 or 40 years ago, with Don Draper in the lobby, those places will continue to be less exciting because not only are they boring today, but they're not going to attract the capital to get much of a change.

'Without naming names, there are many brands that are soulless monuments to how people thought they wanted to travel 40 or 50 years ago and the only reason that you would know what brands they are is by walking outside and looking at the sign. There's nothing about them internally that's a branded experience. They have large tired ballrooms, an F&B that is pretty depressing … and that goes all the way up to what the industry calls upper upscale, which is a segment which, in the developed world, hasn't grown for decades, because people would rather stay in better-priced value accommodation or at the high end. And they will suffer whether there is a big peer-to-peer influence or not, because they are very tired in terms of what they offer.'

Guy Parsons, CEO at easyHotel, could see another sector where Don Draper's junior colleagues were likely to hang out and where the future was looking similarly stressed. He said: 'The old mid-market will just get squeezed and squeezed and squeezed, and people will stay in it because of price or availability or lack of choice, but I think unfortunately it will get squeezed out. Novotel started out as a mid-market and when I was there Posthouse was the default mid-market brand of choice. And it's gone. Whether it's this market or clothing or supermarkets, the mid-market has had to adapt or they've been squeezed out, because you've got all of the limited service brands providing increasingly better products and then you've got all of the lifestyle brands at the top, some of which play in the mid-market space, but absolutely as lifestyle brands to attract people away at that level.

'I can imagine having a conversation with somebody who didn't know the industry and you can say, "Well, you can stay here and it's got a bed, air conditioning and at the other end it's lifestyle, it's experiential and you've got this bit in the middle, which is safe and it's a bit boring." And there is a case for when safe and boring is absolutely right, but I don't think that's enough to sustain it.

'Look at the Ford Mondeo, a mid-market car brand and I can't think of many mid-market car brands which are selling well, because people either want SUVs or super minis and there's a market for sports cars. But that old mid-market Mondeo has gone, because people won't want that. Do I think the mid-market is going to be squeezed? Yes, I do. Does it mean that the big hotel operators are going to suffer? Not necessarily, but they will have to adapt.'

One of the issues facing investors, and indeed facing any of us when making expensive trainer purchases, was the true value of the brand. The hotel sector – the same one that sent out the scent of the brand to unsuspecting journalists in an attempt to make subconscious olfactory connections – rested much of its future on convincing hotel owners that its brands, and the hassle that ensued with sticking to the brand manual, were worth it in hard cash form. A matter that had become more and more pressing, as the soft brands and OTAs provided routes to market that didn't involve the rigid standards that were demanded by the global brands.

Bland and his colleagues had attempted to bring some rigour into the debate with their Brand Margin research, which had FMCG brands as its inspiration. The commoditisation of the hotel room had been an area where, particularly in distribution, the hotel sector had found itself in dangerous territory. Anyone could sell a Mars Bar, after all, and some did it better than others. The brands had to prove that only they could sprinkle the requisite magic dust.

BVA BDRC has taken a different route than straight-up supermarket selling[29]. As Bland said: 'The purpose of a hotel brand, at its core, is to allow the owner of a hotel to increase the number of rooms they sell and the rate at which they sell them. It's no different from the purpose of any other brand – maximise value and increase volume. Marketing 101. Classic measures of brand health look at awareness, usage and preference. These are great measures for assessing performance, but they only tell part of the story. To really understand the true value of a brand, you need to establish the premium that people are willing to pay to choose that brand over the alternatives.

'The abundance of demand data won't do the job in this regard. Big data – such as actual room rates achieved by different brands – won't tell the full story because those rates are influenced by so many factors: seasonality, location, product specifics, and even the skill of the revenue management team. To tell the true story of a brand, we need to strip out those other factors and uncover what the brand itself adds to (or even subtracts from) the price of a room. The only true judges of that are

---

[29]www.bva-bdrc.com/opinions/whats-your-brand-really-worth/

customers, and although they won't tell you directly, we researchers have some tricks to get them to reveal it nonetheless.

'Our methodology was born in the world of FMCG, where products are generally more homogenous and more consistently priced. There is often an intrinsic, underlying price, and we use that to assess the additional revenue a brand commands in percentage terms. We do so by asking respondents to answer with a perceived price that they think other people – and that's crucial – would be prepared to pay. That approach doesn't work with hotel rooms.

'Firstly, they're not as directly comparable. We use four tiers for analysis at BVA BDRC, as we've found that four allows relevance of competition whilst still accounting for practicality of data collection. Yet even assigned to these handy boxes, there is still a huge difference between a Holiday Inn Express room and a room with Tune Hotels. We can't, therefore, assess brands against a common product in the same way that we could for a tin of beans.

'Secondly, they aren't consistently priced. The same product sells for different prices depending on when you book it, where it is, which channel you book through and, in some cases, where in the world you live. This means that, from a research perspective, assigning an intrinsic value will introduce bias at every turn. Brands deliberately offering a more limited service (e.g. easyHotel, ibis Budget) will suffer hugely by comparison, while brands offering a fuller service (Hampton by Hilton) will have their values inflated.

'So, we don't ask respondents to answer with a price; we ask them to answer with a difference. We use a set of boundaries common to each of our four tiers, but phrase the question in terms of comparing a like-for-like product. We also ask about hotels based in different locations, since geography has such a huge bearing on price. The result is a measure of the additional value a hotel brand adds to its own rooms in the minds of customers.'

And who were the lucky winners? In 2017[30], BVA BDRC noted that – and here's the good news for those swelling brand stables – parent brands were becoming more and more prominent. In 2016, IHG began adding 'an IHG Hotel' to those in its stable, with Wyndham following suit, and Accor's advertising campaigns put Accor front and centre, with its 'trading' brands shown at the end. This was proven out that year by Hampton by Hilton in the economy segment, which recorded the highest Brand Margin in 15 of the 19 territories assessed. The power of the 'by Hilton' was strongest when applied to the lower tiers – brands in the economy and mid-market segments can feed off the prestige of the parent.

It happened to a certain extent in the upscale tier, too – Embassy Suites by Hilton, Homewood Suites by Hilton and Canopy by Hilton claimed top-tier ranking in Australia, South East Asia, Russia and Italy, while the Hilton core brand led in Germany and Turkey. Hyatt, Park Plaza and Club Med each led two countries, with Sonesta, AMBA Hotels, Sheraton, Crowne Plaza, Hotel Indigo, Meliá and Okura leading one market apiece.

In the luxury segment, even Hilton declined to deploy the 'by Hilton' tagline, suggesting it saw it adding little value to Conrad and Waldorf Astoria. The latter of these featured twice in the company's list of 'top-ranked luxury brands', as did St Regis and The Luxury Collection.

As Marriott International was certainly hoping, the value of the brands wasn't just in the separate brands, but the collective value of the whole, as the loyalty play attests and we investigate in the next chapter. Parsons agreed that more was definitely the merrier if the global flags wanted to survive in face of the peer-to-peer lodging market.

He said: 'Were I one of the really big operators, I would create a lifestyle brand, because for all of those operators, they're also franchising and you want to have as wide a franchise opportunity as possible. I would guess that they will continue to evolve brands and try to keep up with the consumer.

---

[30]www.bva-bdrc.com/opinions/why-it-matters-who-your-parents-are-even-if-youre-a-hotel/

Some standard brands which you look at and think that the concept is a bit tired, you can evolve them, but if you're going to keep up with the Gen Z and their needs I think it will be different again. There will be a need for hotels to evolve and keep pace with what people want.'

One turns for guidance, as ever, to Mark Essex, director, public policy at KPMG, reminding us all that, when it comes to turndown time, it's about what Mark wants: 'I think hotels should spend less time on their branding and more time on spending a deeper relationship with the customer. They're experts in running hotels, not experts in providing me with an away-from-home accommodation service, which may not be a hotel. They'll get there. The good ones will get there. The people doing the jobs in the hotels will always have jobs. No one needs to worry about their jobs in the hotel industry apart from senior management, but will all the brands exist?'

A third way – the growth of the third-party operators

The brands were on their way to proving themselves, but owners still found themselves furrowing their brows when they looked at their balance sheets. It wasn't that owners mistrusted the brands, exactly, just that they didn't always seem to share the same hopes and dreams. For the brands, the goal was a flag on every hotel and a hotel in every city, airport and promising rural community. For the owner, the goal was a reasonable rate of return. The two did not always come together in perfect alignment, and the suspicion among many owners was that they were paying to further another's business. Failure to address this suspicion allowed the OTAs a route to unhappy owners who balanced the cost of a brand with the cost of paying an OTA – when the 25 per cent commission was compared to having to meet the rigours of a brand, it did not always go the brand's way. When the brands also used the OTAs for distribution, the accusation was that hotel owners were effectively being double charged, which did not benefit the relationship.

Adding to the rumbling undercurrent on the investors' side was the length of contracts, which could go up as high as 50 years for upscale brands such as Four Seasons and Ritz-Carlton. According to HVS, the average contract length in 2014[31] was 21 years, with the group noting that there had been a 'noticeable decrease' in the average length of initial terms across Europe. This was attributed to a number of factors: the proliferation of private equity vehicles in the hotel investment market in recent years, which had placed pressure on operators to offer more competitive, shorter initial terms, although these are generally coupled with more renewal options; the increasing competition among hotel operators seeking to broaden their distribution network; and an increase in hotel investment in emerging markets which, along with the associated risks in such markets, had led both operators and owners to negotiate contracts with shorter terms, to provide the opportunity to exit in the event of disappointing market conditions.

But 21 years was still a fair while, given that hotels were likely to be paying for car parks for flying cars by the end of the contracts' lifespan (no doubt with stringent brand requirements) and there was a feeling among many owners that this was unreasonable, weighting the agreement heavily on the side of the brand, which did not want to be associated with having hotels that were regularly deflagged.

As the global operators grew, so the investors felt more and more outgunned. At the 2015 BLP Hotels Annual Conference, brand dilution was described as 'the biggest challenge to the hotel owner', with friction

[31]www.hvs.com/article/7993-hotel-management-contracts-in-europe

growing between owners and operators amid concerns that brand expansion came at a cost to individual performance.

Dr Edward Wojakovski[32], CEO of The Tonstate Group[33], commented: 'Brand dilution is the biggest challenge to the hotel owner. It creates friction within the family – there is friction between what is important to the owner and the operator. The large operators provide an overall service, but there is a limit to how much a reservations system can do. The only way to deal with it is with an active owner and a well-drafted management contract. A management contract is like a marriage – it has to be reviewed regularly and changes made accordingly.'

Dr Wojakovski acknowledged the role of the brands, adding: 'Generic products require brands. They do cost money, but if you manage it properly it's a safety net. It's an owner's obligation to make sure the brands are successful. It's what my wife says – it's good to have someone you can always blame.'

The shift away from the management contracts that had dominated the sector was highlighted by Giorgio Manenti[34], managing director, Eastdil Secured, who said: 'Lenders were pushing for management contracts in the last cycle – now franchises are allowed.'

This shift towards franchising in Europe saw the growth of the third-party management sector in the region, with companies such as Interstate Hotels & Resorts[35] opening offices to try to replicate their success in the US. This was, the owners felt, a chance for the balance of power to be more

---

[32]Noted in the sector for his preference for letter writing as a form of communication, which is charming and should be encouraged.

[33]Investor in the UK hotel market, not known for raising its head above the parapet, but had a very public spat with then-London Mayor Boris Johnson over the awarding of a contract to a rival hotel without, he said, due transparency. A letter-written spat ensued.

[34]Wowed the crowd at this particular event with photos of the fluffy Eastdil dog. Such was the dominance of the broker at the time that many rivals started to wonder whether kidnapping it might be the smart strategic move.

[35]The group managed 530 properties globally by January 2019 and had made its first move into France.

equally spread as they sought safety in numbers. No more were they the lone owner, but part of a bargaining pool, representing a force to at least catch the attention of the brands, much as the large Reits were able to. The beauty of the third-party management companies was that they were, in the main, brand agnostic.

At Interstate Hotels & Resorts, Steve Terry, VP development, UK, told attendees at the Hotel Operations Conference in 2016: 'We do not insist an owner has a brand – 50 per cent of my signings this year are independent. It's all about what works for the owner – we debadged a hotel last year and the performance increased quite considerably. Not all brands are great, not all add enough value to justify their fees. Our value is purely our fees. From our perspective, that is aligned directly with the owner because a lot of our fees are linked to profit. That's why we have to generate profits for the owner, whereas for the brand the value is in the brand.'

Terry followed this train of thought later that year at the Annual Hotel Conference[36] in Manchester, commenting: 'The brands and owners are mainly aligned, but there's obviously a tension – the brand want it to be a flagship and that costs money. The brand's main concern is whether a hotel meets brand standards, but someone like us has a long-term view – we have to meet projections.'[37]

The brands protested that they were becoming a lot more accommodating, with Tim Walton, VP international hotel development, Marriott International, replying: 'We've all become a lot better on contractual flexibility – we've had to because of more competition in the market. Our interests are aligned with the ownership community, but we are the guardian of the brand. We are a pure-play hotel management and franchising company. It will never be our model to be a long-term owner of real estate. We were relative Johnny-come-latelies to franchising in

---

[36]The sector is always on tour. Just like the Rolling Stones. Just like them.
[37]https://hotelanalyst.co.uk/2016/10/19/flexibility-demanded-from-brands/

the UK, but now we've embraced it. There is a vast range of services that owners and development can take advantage of. Not all brands are created equal and some are viewed as commodities and you get what you pay for. We have the expertise to provide a vast gamut of support. Franchise is probably 95 per cent of our pipeline in the UK. In terms of the services we can provide, it's fairly bespoke.'

Key to the debate was how the hotel brands paid themselves. Contracts typically saw the brands take their fees regardless of the hotels' performance, with a base fee, generally calculated as a percentage of gross operating revenue (ranging typically from 2 per cent to 4 per cent)[38]. HVS said: 'While many owners would argue that an operator should ideally only receive fees based on the profit, not revenue, that the hotel generates, operators have successfully argued that they need to be protected with a certain amount of virtually "guaranteed" income in order for them to be able to subsidise the costs of operating their organisations even during a severe market downturn when hotels' operating profits may be significantly reduced or even, in the worst cases, non-existent for a period of time.'

Some contracts also came with an incentive fee, based on a percentage of the hotel's operating profit. While the base fee encouraged the operator to focus on the top line, the incentive fee ensured that there was also an incentive[39] to control operating costs. There were, of course, other fees and charges, related to items such as centralised reservations, sales and marketing, loyalty programmes, training fees, purchasing costs, accounting or other costs. These fees were, HVS noted, often defined as a percentage – between 1 per cent and 4 per cent – of total revenue or rooms' revenue.

---

[38] www.hvs.com/article/7993-hotel-management-contracts-in-europe
[39] Yes ... that's right.

There was a rising trend observed in the industry whereby operators were accepting lower base fees in return for higher incentive fees of up to 15 per cent of gross operating profit. These were designed to more closely align the operator's interests with those of the owner – to maximise the operating profit of the hotel, regardless of the revenue.

While a fixed incentive fee percentage ranging from 8 per cent to 10 per cent of adjusted gross operating profit was typical, it was becoming increasingly common to have scaled incentive fees. The tendency towards higher or scaled incentive fees, versus higher base fees, rewards effective operators but also provides some protection for the owner's cashflow/ return in the event of poor operator performance or a market downturn.

While the pendulum was swinging towards equality, there were other efficiencies offered by the third-party operators. Back in Manchester, Charles Human, managing director of HVS Hodges Ward Elliott, saw the rise of Interstate and its competitors as driving not only efficiency but also transaction volumes, with third-party managed sites growing in popularity, making up 4 per cent of deals in the UK in 2012/13, but rising to 30 per cent in 2015/16.

Human pointed to branded managed hotels' fees at 10 per cent to 13 per cent of rooms' revenue, while third-party fees were at 10 per cent to 12 per cent. 'The numbers,' he said, 'are compelling'. An increasing number of owners may be feeling compelled, but there were further numbers to be crunched if the third-party fees were added to a franchise. There were also fears that once the third-party managers became huge themselves, they too would lose sight of the individual owners.

David Harper, head of hotel valuations at Hotel Partners Africa and author of *Valuation of Hotels for Investors,* had a few words of caution for hotels looking to compete with Airbnb and the likely impact on these myriad forms of agreement, commenting: 'Airbnb is particularly popular with certain demand demographics, like millennials. Hotels that are trying

to target these groups need to be clever if they are to avoid the impact
that Airbnb has on their trading. By deliberately targeting this younger
tech-savvy generation, the hotel can enhance value while at the same time
reducing the future impact of Airbnb. Of course you don't want to be
alienating existing customers for the sake of appealing to a new group of
customers. What you are after is things that maybe are millennial-driven
but which also have universal appeal. Clearly this will include amenities
such as free WiFi and quality bar offerings, but it will also often include
revamping the form and function of the lobby area, and indeed even
completely changing the food offerings – no more room service on a shiny
silver platter, but deliveries of "to-go food" in environmentally friendly
packaging, so visitors can eat on the run whilst exploring the local area.

'The most worrying thing about Airbnb for the hotel industry is the
trend towards using these disruptors by the younger sections of society.
The consumer loyalty that hotel brands have been working on, that
indeed is almost the basis of their entire offering to hotel owners, is
being undermined at an alarming rate in this key segment of the future
marketplace for accommodation. If a hotel brand has no added value for
this group of consumers, who would just as happily stay in an Airbnb,
how can that hotel brand charge a premium for its management services?
Indeed, why should owners continue to pay for "brand standards" if such
standards are "valueless"? Does this mean that hotel brands will need to
change their offer to hotel owners when taking on new hotel management
agreements? Will they need to be more flexible in the physical structure,
will they need to lower their management charges? Indeed, will there be a
market in 20 years for franchised hotel brands at all – those that have no
management function being supplied, just offering the benefit of a name
that arguably means nothing to key segments in the marketplace?

'Given the love that millennials have for brands, it is likely that hotel
brands will be able to tap into this market, reducing the impressive

Airbnb growth over the longer term, as long as they make themselves relevant to that market. Once again, it will come down to ensuring that the brand offers what the consumers want, and meets their needs and expectations at the very least. Brands that cannot do this will find themselves underperforming in this key demographic, impacting on their overall value, and most likely losing out on hotel opportunities, both management and franchising.'

Vivid imagery around the topic abounded, with brands referred to as '200-lb gorillas'[40] and the value of sticking with the flags as offering 'a single throat to choke'[41]. This malevolence and likelihood towards violence could only mean that the sector was ripe for disruption.

[40]Clive Hillier, co-founder & CEO, Vision Asset Management, on the occasion of the company being sold to Colliers International in 2017, the brokers realising increasingly that they needed more strings to their bows than just selling hotels.
[41]Tom Page, global head of hotels & leisure group, CMS, in 2017, spoken as only a lawyer can.

PART THREE

IT HAS HAPPENED BEFORE, IT WILL HAPPEN AGAIN[1] – WHAT HOTELS DIDN'T LEARN FROM THE LAST ROUND OF DISRUPTION: THE OTAs

In looking at how the hospitality sector had responded to the sharing economy, there were lessons that could be learned – although may not have been – from the last time the sector was shocked by a new entrant prowling around its revenues, something in recent, very much living memory.

High street retailers had seen online decimate their sales, with 2019 seeing the 178-year-old Thomas Cook Group collapse after battling what appeared to be the inevitable. The hotel sector was not exempt from feeling the impact of the shift in distribution. The rise of the OTAs saw hotels pushed into the role of product, while the OTAs took care of the retailing, a position that meant a loss of control not only in terms of cost

---

[1]From 1998 almost-disaster movie *Armageddon*, starring Bruce Willis. Something similar was said in Ecclesiastes. And by J.M. Barrie in *Peter Pan*. Apparently we're not a learning species.

of distribution, but also about how the consumer viewed the product. In allowing the intangible – the fleeting room night – to be commoditised, rooms had been stripped to their essence: location and price, with the hawkish eye of the consumer needing to see multiple justifications as to why they should pay a penny more for anything else.

The OTAs crept up on an unwitting hotel sector in much the same way as the Internet and its selling potential crept up on most retailers. Kate Nicholls, CEO at UK Hospitality, said: 'Retail got seduced by online and they didn't realise what was happening. Retailers started to have more and more concessions, which meant losing control of your customer and your relationship with your customer. Concessions within department stores mean that your loyalty stops being to House of Fraser and lies more with the concession. With the move online, shops just became a literal window and you ordered online, so you are again one stage removed from your customer. Delivery of your product and delivery of your service is now in the hands of someone else. Once you are so far down that route, you can't close the stable door after the horse has bolted – it has become part and parcel of people's everyday life.'

The seductive whisper of the OTAs began in 1996, with the launch of Microsoft Expedia Travel Services, but the offering didn't gain traction until the 9/11 terror attacks of 2001 and then later, during the 2008 downturn, when hotels found themselves up a certain creek without a certain way of selling their excess hotel rooms. Hotel rooms that ceased to exist the morning after, the very mirage of lost revenue sailing off into the night. Those needing to fill rooms were prepared to take anything, training the consumer to wait until the last minute until booking, seeding booking habits that were to become entrenched, which in turn then limited the ability of hotels to forecast their own business.

At first, it was all going so well. The leading OTAs – Expedia Group, The Priceline Group, Ctrip, and later the metasearch engines such as

Trivago, to pluck some random names – picked up distressed rooms, or blocks of rooms, sold them on and the hotels saw guests and revenue they might otherwise have not garnered. Hotels were happy to pay commissions of 5–10 per cent on the sales and benefit from the Billboard Effect, where they enjoyed the OTAs' marketing reach without having to invest themselves.

As horror stories are wont to play out, it was all smooth sailing in the beginning. We've all seen it before: the backpackers accepted a lift in the strange van and no one expected to be axed up in act two. Then, edging behind the sofa, commissions started increasing – to between 15–30 per cent for larger hotel chains and even higher for smaller players – and the hotels had somehow failed to come up with digital strategies of their own to counter the threat. For the grumpy hotel investors, irritated at the cost of the brands, OTAs were offering another route to market and, finally, the chance of a competitive stick to beat the flags with. The OTAs started to pick up independent hotels who looked at the cost of them and, comparing it with the cost of management or franchise agreements, couldn't fit a cigarette paper in between.

Hotels, of course, did nothing to help themselves, colluding in their own suffering in an attempt to regain control of how they were stacked on the OTAs' shelves. In 2002, several hotel chains imposed rate parity clauses to prevent merchants underselling them, having become peeved at discounts being offered on their own products. Of course, this also meant that hotels couldn't undercut the rates offered at the OTAs and so everyone was locked in a dance of differentiation, with the OTAs using their superior marketing firepower to sell the story that they were the ones offering the bargains – they were certainly the ones offering the most choice.

Fortunately, before either party could think of any other ways to dig themselves in deeper, authorities across Europe started to notice the clauses and ask some troubling questions about how the consumer was benefitting from these rate agreements. Followers of French politics might be interested to note that, before becoming president, Emmanuel Macron, who was at the time France's Minister of Economy, Industry and Digital Affairs, successfully drove through a law named after himself, stating that when entering into contracts with OTAs, 'the hotelier is free to consent to any customer discounts or tariff advantage of any kind whatsoever'. Macron was encouraged by a two-year battle led by Accor and hotel employer union UMIH to remove the pricing parity clauses enforced by France's three largest OTAs: Booking.com, Expedia and HRS.

Once the Macron law had raised the profile of the debate in 2015, other jurisdictions followed, most notably in Germany, where the Bundeskartellamt (national competition regulator) ruled that such clauses violated German and European competition law. Italy, Belgium and Sweden followed suit and in 2017 the network of European competition authorities – including the European Commission – decided to keep the online hotel booking sector under review[2].

Was this really progress? The OTAs held a lot of power after having caught hotels on the digital hop – many of those at the coalface had noted that the rate parity clauses in contracts were rarely tested and hotels did what they were told. The OTAs did have other weapons in their armoury, with punishments administered for naughty hotels who found themselves pushed down search rankings if they didn't offer up their best prices. There were also fears that the OTAs' fondness for predatory advertising and dubious panic messaging – 'LAST ROOM REMAINING! OFFER FOR TODAY ONLY' – was more dangerous than rate parity.

---

[2]www.europarl.europa.eu/doceo/document/E-8-2017-005112-ASW_EN.html?redirect#def3

And had hotels noticed the death of rate parity anyway? In 2017, the European Competition Network[3] co-ordinated efforts across 10 member states, sending questionnaires to 16,000 hotels, 20 OTAs, 11 metasearch websites and 19 large hotel chains, with the conclusion that allowing OTAs to use narrow parity clauses, and then prohibiting OTAs from using them altogether, had 'generally improved conditions for competition and led to more choice for consumers'.

The study found that 47 per cent of the hotels that responded to the electronic survey did not know that Booking.com and Expedia had changed or removed their parity clauses. This figure was lower in France and Germany, at 30 per cent. Of those hotels that knew about the changes, the majority said they had not acted upon them in any way.

The reasons most frequently given for not price differentiating were that the hotel saw no reason to treat its OTA partners differently; the hotel's OTA contract did not allow it to price differentiate; fear of penalisation by OTAs to which the hotel did not give the lowest price; the difficulty of managing different prices on different OTAs; and not wanting the hotel's website to appear as more expensive than those of the OTAs.

For those that did price differentiate between OTAs, the most frequent reason given was to increase the hotel's visibility on a particular OTA. In France and Germany, a higher share of respondents said that they had price differentiated between OTAs. However, this difference was not confirmed by pricing data scraped by the monitoring working group from OTA websites, which showed no significant variation between any of the participating member states.

Charlie Osmond, chief tease at Triptease, a platform designed to help hotels drive direct bookings, saw a creeping awareness on the part of

[3]http://ec.europa.eu/competition/ecn/hotel_monitoring_report_en.pdf Hotel accommodation was not among the products covered by the Commission's E-commerce Sector Inquiry

hotels, dragged towards the realisation that the Internet was likely to catch on and it was potentially going to cost more than it was worth if an attempt wasn't made to seize back control. Osmond said: 'Hoteliers are growing much more aware of the extent of their parity problems and the link between those problems and their direct revenue. Leaky onward distribution, particularly of rates intended for wholesale, is a huge issue that will only be fixed by a fairly radical change of approach from the hotel industry. Moving to dynamic rates and taking a more active role in managing partners are two of the more important steps that hotels can take.

'Where we see a really positive relationship between hotels and OTAs is where the hotel takes a very proactive approach to working out the particular type of guest they want to attract through an OTA, and then ensures they have a robust strategy in place for acquiring the rest of their guests either through their direct channel or through other means. Hotels performing this kind of channel-by-channel analysis, who are constantly adjusting their inventory and availability in order to acquire their ideal revenue mix, are the ones we see working best with OTAs.

'Implicit in this though is the amount of time and effort that goes into maintaining a good relationship that doesn't cannibalise the hotel's direct revenue. What's becoming clear is that OTAs are no longer a straightforward distribution channel for hotels. The major OTAs have global brands to maintain, and that means that they aren't always going to act in a hotel's best interests – from the hotel's point of view. For instance, if we take the issue of unpackaged wholesale rates, where rates intended for inclusion in tours or packages are sold directly to consumers via OTAs, we can see that major OTAs are tending to exacerbate the problem for the hotels involved by pulling those cheap rates through to their own sites rather than work with hotels to solve the root issue.'

For hotels, which were trying to do any number of things on top of trying to run hotels, the pressure from pure-play distribution companies was intense, largely because they were being outgunned. Osmond pointed out that 'hoteliers have learned that OTAs are winning for a reason' and that reason was that they knew more about e-commerce and how to market. As Lennert de Jong, commercial director at citizenM, said earlier: 'I'm guilty myself, I book on Booking because it's so frickin' simple. The OTAs might have commoditised the purchase of a hotel room, but they have created a transparency. I can do all sorts of searches on an OTA and I can see what I want and what I can get and what people say about it.' The OTAs had perfected booking with just a few taps, using revolutions such as saving your credit card details. And contact details. And other things that the hotel companies also had access to but on which they had failed to join the dots.

Hotels started to adopt similar strategies to the OTAs, forcing themselves to be sullied in the world of commerce, so far from the silver service and damask tablecloths, and try to use OTAs strategically, to use their marketing heft to their advantage and reach consumers that they wouldn't otherwise get a chance to touch. In 2018, Booking Holdings was estimated to have spent over $1 billion[4] with Google in one quarter, a spend that hotels could not hope to keep up with, but hoped to benefit from. This, Osmond warned, was not always the case, noting that it took a while for hotels to appreciate the extent to which many OTA bookers were not incremental, 'and were actually a result of their distribution partners cannibalising their own traffic by, for instance, bidding on branded search terms. It's taken time for hoteliers to realise that OTAs are in many cases no longer the positive incremental addition to their business that they

---

[4] www.cnbc.com/2018/11/05/travel-giant-booking-spent-1-billion-on-google-ads-in-the-quarter.html

once were'. Yes, those brand names on which the operators were staking their futures were being snapped up by the highest bidders.

Over and over, the hotels had to battle against a single-focus industry while also having to remember to change the beds. Osmond commented on the 'sheer rate of change' at the OTAs, against the distribution position at hotels, which they have had to adapt to going 'from a yearly cycle of managing their distribution to a daily – even hourly – one. OTAs have always been online businesses, whereas hoteliers have had to learn how to become digital experts as well as hospitality professionals. It's only very recently that a true online-led mentality has come into the culture of some hotels, with roles like "product manager" making the leap over from the tech industry to hospitality.

'As an industry, the hotel sector remained unusually reliant on particular systems and models of software after other e-commerce industries moved on to leaner, more iterative systems. The complex web of GDS, PMS, CMS, CRS means that rapid change hasn't always been easy, even for the savviest data-led hotels. Indeed, the proliferation of systems means that combining data into a "single source of truth" is actually pretty difficult to achieve for a hotel – a factor that perhaps contributed to the slightly delayed realisation of the potential harms of OTA reliance. OTAs were, and still are, an excellent channel for acquiring incremental revenue outside the reach of a hotel's individual marketing budget. They played a crucial role in allowing hotels to benefit from the advent of e-commerce and enabled widespread distribution at a fraction of the cost of traditional channels at that time. It is the overreaching of this rule and the contingent rapid increase in commission that has caused the imbalance we currently see in the industry.'

Each hotel company had to look at how they fit the OTAs into their overall distribution pattern and, for a small number of SMEs, this meant handing over their sales and marketing budget and going 100 per cent with the OTAs. For de Jong, it is about embracing the reality of the situation, but making sure that staff are aware of the cost to the hotel of bookings that come from the OTAs, motivating them to drive direct bookings instead. He said: 'We have done a horrible job in the hotel sector of training people that they should give people a better deal on the phone. You can call a hotel and explain that you should pay less because they are not paying a commission for the booking, but they don't offer you a lower rate.'

He also warned against the habit by many hotels of treating those who landed on their doorsteps via an OTA as second-class citizens – a curious strategy for businesses wanting to encourage repeat bookings. But a quick survey of guests who find themselves looking out over car parks or being woken by the vibrations from the lift shaft will often reveal a third-party distributor in their shameful purchase history and the emotional response of many hotels is that these guests should be punished.

De Jong was more liberal, commenting that he didn't care how the customer wanted to book – citizenM instead ran a dynamic price product 'and if you have a lot of people who come back to you and you're not fighting with them as to how they book, you drop your prices.

'In my eyes, Marriott and Hilton are an OTA and that's what they're doing, they're fighting with the other two OTAs and you're hearing more and more noise coming from the owner side of the community. The OTAs are there to put the best product in front of you and I don't think the OTAs believe the big box chains are doing that. At citizen, we are owners. In the end, we are trying to reach people – how they book I cannot control. I am not going to bet citizenM's future on the failure of Booking or Expedia. You have to look at where the costs go. We've made certain agreements with the OTAs that are more long term. We are channel agnostic, we don't want to fight with the customer, we like them as a customer, we're not going to say: "Thank you for coming, but screw you for using an OTA".'

'Screw you' was the least of the language being thrown around behind the scenes at hotels, as they appreciated that they would never be able to turn themselves into technology companies but needed another lever to pull, something that the OTAs didn't have. The answer came, in part, out of the Office of Fair Trading's investigation into rate parity antics between IHG, Booking.com and Expedia in the UK in 2012. The investigation was closed after the three agreed that it was possible to offer discounts to closed groups. Loyalty schemes, to not coin a phrase.

The good news for the consumer – those oft-forgotten participants being shoved into a room near the lift shaft – was that someone had their back and had noted that, while the online distribution was foxing businesses, there might be other victims too. Ann Pope, senior director in the OFT's services, infrastructure and public markets group, concluded: 'The travel industry, fuelled by the Internet, has seen significant changes in recent years, and we want to ensure those changes continue to work in consumers' interests. That is why we are pleased to have secured this outcome, which, by allowing OTAs and hotels to offer discounts, should increase competition and mean travellers across Europe can benefit from reductions on hotel accommodation throughout the UK. By shopping around, people can compare the different discounts offered by hotels and OTAs, and ensure they get the best deal.'[5]

Onwards to loyalty schemes and the brands were quick to start pushing their benefits; largely that members who booked direct could enjoy cheaper rates. For decades, these loyalty schemes had been sitting around irritating people trying to enjoy a speedy check-in. It was Holiday Inn, which pioneered hotel franchises, that also led the way with loyalty programmes, launching Priority Club Rewards in 1983. By the end of 2018, the programme had more than 100 million

---

[5]https://webarchive.nationalarchives.gov.uk/20140402182607/http://www.oft.gov.uk/news-and-updates/press/2014/06-14

members, or the equivalent of 296 Icelands. A pretty decent contact list for filling your hotels. In 2016, Holiday Inn owner InterContinental Hotels Group launched 'Your Rate' by IHG Rewards Club, giving lower rates to loyalty members who booked direct and following the trend set by Hilton, which earlier that year had launched a discounted loyalty rate and a global advertising campaign – including on television, not frequent advertising ground for hotels – under the tagline 'Stop Clicking Around'.

Cindy Estis Green, CEO and co-founder at Kalibri Labs, said: 'The brands have had loyalty programmes in place for many years, as did the airlines, well before the rise of the OTAs. I suspect they have evolved in response to the steep adoption of all things digital and the consumer's changing behaviour in response to everything moving to online. I would not say it's anything directly connected to the OTAs as much as connected to the broader move to digital, tech and online activities in all spheres of life, not just travel.'

Everything in the garden was rosy. The hotel companies frolicked around claiming that, from now on, they were going to show restraint when using the OTAs and they finally had something to respond with to their owners, who had started to use the OTAs as a stick to beat them with. It couldn't last. The OTAs started a whispering campaign in full voice, claiming that the loyalty programmes were, in fact, costing owners more than they were saving on OTA fees. Later in 2016, Expedia made the argument that hotel owners were paying the price for the direct-book programmes, commenting that reduced exposure on the OTAs' sites and high loyalty programme costs was leading to a fall in revenue per room of 8 per cent.[6]

No no, the hotels said – direct bookings were 9 per cent more profitable than bookings that had come via the OTAs, according to a study by Kalibri

---

[6]https://hotelanalyst.co.uk/2016/06/06/direct-battle-in-full-swing/

Labs, which reported that, when factoring in ancillary spend, profitability could be almost 18 per cent better than with OTA-booked guests. The study included commissions, transaction fees, loyalty fees, and any other direct channel costs.

The report pointed to falling costs for direct bookings over time, when, as the loyalty roster grows, marketing costs are reduced against the cost of an OTA booking, which remained constant no matter how often it was repeated.

The study added that higher net ADR suggested that while some loyalty guests who had previously paid full rates were taking advantage of the discounts, many were not. The study concluded that third-party business from OTAs, metasearch, wholesalers and traditional travel agencies could be an important factor but that a healthy balance was all.

There were rumours of retaliation by some OTAs, who were playing with rankings and also 'dimming' certain hotels in their search results. In 2019, the Leibniz Centre for European Economic Research in Mannheim, alongside Télécom ParisTech and the Düsseldorf Institute for Competition Economics, published a report[7] that seemed to point to platforms punishing hotels for listing their rooms more cheaply elsewhere.

In a continuation of the rate parity debate from back in the day, the study found that if a hotel charged a lower price on a competing platform or on its own website, this resulted in a worse ranking of the hotel in the platform's recommended search results. This held regardless of whether a country had price parity clauses or not.

The greater the price difference between competing platforms, the greater the effect on a hotel's positioning in the platforms' search results. As a consequence, hotels with lower prices on competing channels were

---

[7]www.zew.de/en/presse/pressearchiv/hotels-erhalten-schlechtere-rankings-bei-niedrigeren-preisen-auf-anderen-webseiten/

less visible than those that did not undercut rates. This in turn had an influence on the pricing decision of hotels and could reduce price differentiation across all channels.

Reinhold Kesler, co-author of the study, said: 'By considering price differentials, OTAs make their recommended search results dependent on factors that are relevant to maximising the platforms' profits, but which are not necessarily in the customer's interest.'

However, this strategy entailed certain risks. On the one hand, platforms could influence hotels' pricing decisions across all distribution channels when optimising their search results in this way. This can to a certain extent be regarded as a substitute for price parity clauses, which were banned by competition authorities and lawmakers in several European countries. On the other hand, this can reduce the search quality for users if the search results are not in line with consumer interests.

Kesler said: 'It would be desirable for OTAs to better inform consumers about how they calculate their rankings labelled as "Recommended" or "Our top picks". Consumers could then make a more elaborate decision as to whether they want to actually follow the recommendation. This could in turn improve search quality for users and possibly also eliminate the anti-competitive effects of such platform strategies.'

Points don't always mean prizes: how loyalty schemes lost their allure

In a 'friends close/enemies closer' move, the two parties started buddying up, with the OTAs offering additional services – revenue management, sipping from their data pools – as a means to make themselves indispensable. At Expedia Group's Explore '18 event in Las Vegas in 2018, CEO Mark Okerstrom told delegates – made up of his suppliers: car rental companies and, well, hotels – 'If Amazon is the global platform for the ordering of consumer goods, then Expedia is the global platform for the physical movement of people.' Not the most relaxing comment ever made, given the trauma suffered throughout the publishing world by the distribution shift triggered by Amazon. Okerstrom added, no more cheerily: 'For the last five years we have been on a journey to change our relationship with the chains. If you think of all the ways that we can work together with data and revenue management, I am confident that we can work together – not partnering can be an existential threat.'

Nothing like throwing 'existential threat' into the mix to really warm the soul. But the OTAs – and their rival distributors – aware that they too were caught in the endless chase for scale, had been wooing hotels, in particular independents, but also small chains, seeking to offer their loyalty discounts through their own websites. It seemed to remove the point of the schemes in the first place, although Expedia thought not, arguing that it was extra customer contact and more names for those loyalty lists.

It was at this point that the difference between 'loyalty programmes' and 'reward programmes' needed to be called out, as customers were at risk of being loyal to discounts and nothing more, the shallow idiots. After all, said James Bland, director at BVA BDRC: 'There are very, very few brands which inspire love and loyalty.'

Estis Green argued: 'It appears that consumers are looking for more than just a game of points-for-stays. The benefits that accrue for a hotel loyalty guest are those that make the travel experience more convenient or tend to the traveller's "creature comforts", which has a much bigger impact overall and means that it's not only for the road warrior and high-frequency travellers. Anyone travelling wants the convenience of mobile check-in or keyless entry or the ability to find out about local attractions or restaurants to help in their trip planning. If the loyalty programme, driven by the brand loyalty app, provides these benefits but you have to be a member to get them, this goes well beyond the old system of collecting points to drive membership and retention.'

Nicholls agreed: 'Loyalty programmes are the way to regain control of the customer relationship, certainly it helps with OTAs, that's the way to get control of the customer data back. I don't think customers are as brand loyal. The cleverer companies are using loyalty not on price, but on additional benefits that you get as part of the service that make it part of the difference. So the OTAs might be a room-only price, the loyalty programme will give you breakfast, bathrobes, slippers, access to spas, or fruit or a bottle of wine in the room. They can be a bit cleverer in their marketing if they want to provide that idea of a personal host.'

The question of data was one that also appealed to Estis Green. Knowledge, one hears, is power; there was gold to be mined from data. She said: 'The driving force is the digital and tech marketplace and that means using data more effectively and a shift in all sectors – not just travel – to AI and predictive modelling to figure out what consumers want so their needs can be met more effectively. So, I say that personalisation is a good example of the trend going forward in terms of use of data to improve each step in the travel journey.'

If the thought of all that data crunching gave hotels the yips, Frits van Paasschen, author, citizenM advisory board, former Starwood Hotels & Resorts president and CEO, pointed out that it didn't have to be that hard to become closer to the guest. He said: 'When we launched the Ambassador programme at Starwood, going back about 10 years, the first thing we did was call the people who disproportionately contributed to our profitability and found out what they wanted. We found that if you travel 50, 100, 150 nights per year, then a lot of what you want is pretty basic stuff. If you are allergic to down feathers you want to know that's not going to be in the room. Another might be a vegan who doesn't appreciate the cheese plate, another is someone who says, "Look, I'm just going to be in the room for seven hours, don't give me a suite upgrade, I'm just going to spend the time turning off the lights, but on the weekend, when I'm going on my anniversary or I'm taking my family out, by all means upgrade me." Personalisation is a combination of things, one of which is literally a personalised service. Technology and scale can offer ways to do that better than a traditional innkeeper might have done years ago just by being a good hotelier. The combination of that kind of recognition and a good understanding of what individual preferences are is something that could and should be implemented systematically across hotel systems, and it's absolutely a way that the larger hotel chains should be able to compete. It's just taking them a very long time to get there.'

For those who were not travelling 150 nights a year just to wear their thumbs out on light switches, there needed to be something more thrilling than just accruing an awful lot of points in multiple schemes, which seemed to be the prevailing trend among loyalty programmes.

Marieke Dessauvagie, hotel consultant at Colliers International, said: 'The traditional loyalty programmes won't have much effect in the long term; guests want to see direct benefits instead of earning points, which in the long run, maybe in two years, they can get one night off. Guests want more benefits now. Hotels have a way to go to achieve that.'

Robin Sheppard, chairman at Bespoke Hotels, was similarly cautious, adding: 'I think if I was a major hotel group with a huge loyalty programme, I would really be nervous. Because there's only so many ways that you can keep inventing the product and get the kind of loyalty that you're looking for.'

And all that came with a cost, but for the larger players it was mandatory. In 2019, Accor announced plans to invest €225 million over two years on loyalty, partnerships and brand marketing, to improve customer engagement and help it compete with the other global hotel operators, part of which would include the launch of loyalty programme 'All'[8]. The company described this as 'a fully integrated global platform, integrating rewards, services, and experiences across our entire ecosystem to bring value to everyday life, whether you work, live or play' (and anyone who's spent a day in a typical dungeon conference room will know that 'live' is not always a given...).

Sébastien Bazin, Accor's chairman and CEO, said at the group's FY 2018 results presentation that he wanted to see: 'Better frequency, better usage, better interaction. Our loyalty programme is 50 million members today, it was 25 million only four years ago. We have many more loyalty members every year, but it's only a good thing if they are increasing the numbers of bookings going through the system – and they are not enough. It means nothing if you don't engage in a more frequent manner. We need the 30 per cent of bookings from loyalty to be 45 per cent' – more, he said, like his American competitors.

He added: 'Let's stop being transactional – what we have talked about is points, but people want something they can't buy. Those days of [points] have shifted enormously and what people want today is not credit – they want to be identified, they want passion. We are spending round €150 million in marketing every year; that's €750 million spent over the last five years I have been CEO.' But, he said, the one marketing act anyone could name when pressed was the group's 10-year deal to rename the Paris indoor concert hall and sports arena Palais Omnisports de Paris Bercy as the AccorHotels arena, at a cost of €4.5 million per year. Oh, he was sure that the rest of the money had been well spent, but 'it's just that I don't remember and I guess that others don't either. We have to be bold, we have to be audacious, we have to shout that the days of Accor not

---

[8]https://press.accorhotels.group/h1unveils-new-lifestyle-loyalty-programh1bringing-augmented-hospitality-to-life/

being present are over. We are the biggest hotel operator on the planet. We have to show who we are and that will have an impact on converting loyalty members to active, to increasing RevPAR.'

Bazin told investors that the group was no longer working on any M&A projects[9], but that instead 'I am focusing 99.9 per cent of my time on what matters most: team, brands, loyalty and guests. We are going from product into client lifestyle.' And, before the company's owners went into a catatonic spiral about how much this spiffy new loyalty programme was going to cost, Bazin said that deep discounting on member rates would not be a feature. Instead, experience would be the focus; specifically, guests' passions, which the company identified as 'dining and culinary, entertainment and sport'.

For Accor, the move was a significant one, undertaken at the same time that it dropped the 'hotels' from its name. To reference Pinocchio, the company was acting like a grown-up, real boy. A consumer brand to play with the other brands and step out from the realms of the hospitality sector to become something bigger. The group wanted to move into what it called 'the next generation of guest engagement', where it offered services that consumers used every day, outside the world of hotels; a next generation of guest engagement, but in payment, credit cards, retail, food delivery, airlines and car rental, making the company part of daily life.

Accor was not the only company to revamp its loyalty scheme. It wasn't even the only one to do so that quarter, with Marriott International launching the programme it had created in the crucible of its merger with Starwood Hotels & Resorts, an offering it called Bonvoy[10], a name that conjured the lazy speech patterns of a teenager, but that was at least quick to type. And why such a distinctive name? Because the loyalty

---

[9]Obviously no one believed this for even the slightest of moments.
[10]http://news.marriott.com/2019/01/marriott-international-announces-marriott-bonvoy-the-new-name-of-its-loyalty-program/

programmes were now entities of their own. The consumer face of the B2B operator. This programme had 120 million members at launch and, like Accor, the company was trying to move consumers away from seeing the schemes as frequency programmes whereby they could get discounts and more as programmes that engendered loyalty. With fun, free stuff that no one else could access.

Happily for the hotel sector, the decision by both companies to go big on their loyalty programmes also came with a side of puerile entertainment, much to the relief of all observers, who needed a dash of fluff with the earnest chats about customer engagement. Accor, having learned from the success of its AccorHotels arena deal, became the principal partner and official jersey sponsor of Paris Saint-Germain Football Club[11], a move Bazin said would see 1 million jerseys a year printed with the Accor logo. The news of this deal came a week after Marriott International announced that Bonvoy would feature on the shirts of Manchester United. A match was due between the two later that month, pitting one loyalty programme against the other in the beautiful game. And, in a move worthy of soap writers, the date was set for the last day of the hotel sector's key conference[12].

Off the pitch, there were those for whom a branded shirt and the chance to meet footballers would never be enough to engender true devotion and, with an eye to the future, Mark Essex, director, public policy at KPMG, had some ideas about what could be done to make him feel much, much more loyal. Essex said: 'I think hotels are missing a trick. What they should do is say, "Mark, whenever you are away from home, we'll find you somewhere to stay". Instead of having a loyalty scheme to encourage you to come back, we will own your hotel stays for you. So whenever you're away, if we have a hotel there it's much cheaper for us to use that one; if we don't, we'll

---

[11]Where Accor CEO Bazin had previously been CEO, causing many an All member to swoon in relief that he hadn't been big in sewerage in a past life.
[12]Marriott International won 2–0. But it ain't over.

arrange it on your behalf. And maybe that will be through an Airbnb, but basically just tell us when you're travelling and you'll never have to worry about it again and we'll put you up near the CBD or near your address. If we can't get you into the centre, we'll get a car to take you there. Which is effectively what my secretary did for me; if the hotel group did it for me, I'd need less of a secretary. I'd go upstream and take those business clients and if one hotel is busy you just move them around; you don't have to ring up the secretary and rebook, you just email the Uber driver and give them a different address. And if you do want a specific hotel, then you just say so and pay more.'

Essex reiterated the opinion that the greatest damage caused by the OTAs was not the inserting of a line of cost to make your eyes water, but turning hotel rooms into a box on a shop shelf in the eyes of the purchaser, describing them as a 'commodity product, not a branded product. If I was them, I wouldn't major on their own brands, I'd go upstream and own the customer. They even admit it, because they call themselves four star and five star – that's the real brand'.

The other operators drew attention to the success of their loyalty programmes. By 2018, Hilton Worldwide CEO Chris Nassetta said[13] that members accounted for approximately 60 per cent of system-wide occupancy, which was, as one would imagine, pretty nifty, but also that those members were 'actively engaged'. He said: 'Five or six years ago I think we would have said we probably had 15 per cent to 20 per cent of that number that were really engaged. Today, 50 per cent, so half of the 42 million. We could auto-enrol the whole world if we wanted. We could have one billion people if we wanted. But it's how do we get people in the programme that we can get engaging with us and staying with us and buying our products.'

---

[13]https://seekingalpha.com/article/4240758-hilton-worldwide-holdings-hlt-ceo-chris-nassetta-q4-2018-results-earnings-call-transcript

Nassetta said that the company was 'focused on driving direct relationships and direct business. Our web-direct channels remain the fastest-growing channels that we have and growing at a much faster rate than OTA channels'.

A strong brand with a clear message continued to have heft. At the group's capital markets day in 2019, Whitbread described Premier Inn[14] as having 'best-in-class direct distribution' with 97 per cent direct bookings, against, it said, Travelodge with 89 per cent, Holiday Inn Express with 80 per cent and Ibis with 80 per cent. OTA bookings, Whitbread CEO Alison Brittain said, had decreased from 9 per cent to just 3 per cent in three years, with the group seeing a 15 per cent decrease in marketing costs per room sold due to digital market effectiveness.

Brittain described Premier Inn as having a 'unique' model and was critical of the move to asset light in which the sector had been revelling, commenting: 'Key value-creating areas in the hotel industry are predominantly under separate ownership ... leading to inconsistent priorities and competing interests and limiting ability to achieve domestic scale'.

In contrast, she said, Premier Inn's vertical integration enabled 'consistent priorities in all value-creating activities, supported end-to-end focus on quality, service and value for money, and provided domestic scale to ensure customer proposition delivered at a low cost', all of which meant a 'clear structural advantage over sub-scale competitor set'. They stuck to their knitting and the consumer stuck with them, to paraphrase. Did they have a loyalty scheme? Not so much.

By 2019, had the loyalty strategy worked, or did everyone just feel dirty after getting a cheap deal on their off-the-shelf room? According

---

[14]www.whitbread.co.uk/media/press-releases/2019/13-02-2019

to Kalibri Labs[15], a study of hotel companies' initial campaigns to attract loyalty members and drive direct bookings over a period from January 2016 through August 2018 found that they had either stabilised or strengthened the growth rate of bookings via their own website – the so-called Brand.com sites – primarily by growing loyalty programmes. Meanwhile, bookings growth for OTAs during this period either held steady or decelerated, signalling, the company said, a shift for the hotel industry.

Airbnb v. OTA: a blurring of battle lines

According to the study, bookings made via Brand.com and those made directly with a hotel property accounted for 23 per cent and 29 per cent of all bookings made between August 2017 and August 2018, respectively. Meanwhile, OTAs represented 15 per cent[16] of all bookings, trending closer to group bookings at 14 per cent. Additionally, bookings made via voice channels stood at 8 per cent, producing in total roughly six in 10 room nights through direct channels. Yes, for all the huffing and puffing, hotels still had control of more of their bookings than the OTAs.

The report also found that net room revenues recorded from OTAs was lower in the long term due to typical OTA commission rates of 15 per cent. Overall, the report found that direct bookings were, on average, 12.5 per cent more profitable than bookings made through OTAs.

'In the beginning, [brands] were all offering discounts on bookings, sometimes up to 10 per cent, to entice people to sign up to be loyalty

---

[15]https://static1.squarespace.com/static/5637877ee4b0e3bf6b1a4aec/t/5c45f32703ce64e 2d2130998/1548088106568/Kalibri_Book+Direct_Campaigns_2018_Full+Report+BDSR.pdf
[16]And yet to hear the hotel companies freaking out, you'd think it was 85 per cent.

members,' said Estis Green. 'In the last 2.5 years, almost all brands have substantially updated their apps to offer keyless entry, more features, mobile check-in and different services such as those. All these benefits only apply when booking through the brand's app or as a loyalty member, and those things were not in place in the beginning.'

Add into that the negotiating clout that the spate of consolidation in the sector had driven and the hotels were beginning to feel that they had all the answers to the questions the owners were throwing at them. Tim Ramskill, managing director, head of EMEA equity research, said that scale was easier to achieve through asset-light growth and this scale could then be used as a bargaining chip to achieve better commission rates from the OTAs. And attractive commission rates made the operators more attractive to owners. Scale begat scale in a virtuous circle.

Enter Airbnb, announcing in 2018[17] that it was ruining everyone's day with its offering to list independent hotels at advantageous rates. Dessauvagie said: 'Airbnb is introducing services – loyalty, trips, the business segment – they are working more towards being a disruptor to the OTAs. They are allowing more hotels. If Airbnb remains focused on homesharing, there is a limit to their impact. There will always be people who would rather stay in a hotel. Once they start to act more like an OTA their impact will be higher – but they will only be an OTA.

'The OTAs will also resist in the first instance. The major difference between Airbnb and the OTAs is that Airbnb also charges a fee to the guests and is able to reduce the fee that they charge to the host. If they did that for hotels as well it would make it very interesting and attractive to hotels. OTAs have to respond by either making their loyalty programme more attractive or their offering more attractive.'

Airbnb, meanwhile, continued to show all the classic symptoms of being a wannabe OTA, while denying it with vigour. In 2019, the company

---

[17] www.airbnb.co.uk/help/article/1526/what-are-airbnb-s-standards-for-hotels

appointed as global head of transportation Fred Reid[18], founding CEO of Virgin America; president of Delta Airlines, who led the formation of SkyTeam global alliance; president and COO of Lufthansa German Airlines in 1996; and co-architect of Star Alliance.

Reid said: 'I'm excited to work with [Airbnb] to tackle the third part of the travel experience: how you get there. Whether in the air or on the ground, there are tremendous opportunities to create products and forge partnerships with other companies that make travel easier and even fun.'

The platform said: 'Airbnb's mission is to create a world where anyone can belong anywhere. To advance our mission, we are focused on reimagining travel by building an end-to-end travel platform that combines where you stay, what you do, and how you get there, all in one place.'

Airbnb's co-founder, CEO and head of community Brian Chesky said: 'There was a time when getting on a plane was a magical trip of its own, but over the years, how you get to where you're going has become an experience we endure, not enjoy. We believe that needs to change.'

Chesky said that the homesharing company was 'not interested in building our own airline or creating just another place on the Internet where you can buy a plane ticket. We're going to explore a broad range of ideas and partnerships that can make transportation better. We haven't settled on exactly what those will look like… but there is a tremendous opportunity to improve the transportation experience for everyone.'

Take that description to the online consumer and they might just call it an OTA. The waters were muddied further when, shortly after the appointment, it acquired last-minute booking platform HotelTonight[19] in an estimated $400 million deal that Airbnb said would help it reimagine travel 'by building an end-to-end travel platform that combines where you stay, what you do, and how you get there, all in one place.'

[18]https://press.airbnb.com/fred-reid-joins-airbnb-as-global-head-of-transportation/
[19]https://press.airbnb.com/airbnb-signs-agreement-to-acquire-hoteltonight/

Chesky said: 'A big part of building an end-to-end travel platform is serving every guest, whether they plan their trip a year or a day in advance. Working with the incredible team at HotelTonight, we will offer guests an unparalleled last-minute travel experience that provides unique, memorable hospitality on every trip, on any schedule, at any time.'

The transaction was the group's largest acquisition to date, following 2017's $300 million purchase of Luxury Retreats, which Airbnb said had helped to bring new guests to Airbnb, 'making our community larger and stronger'. Airbnb said that, once those new guests came to Airbnb, 'they're returning to book with our Home hosts; in fact, nearly 90 per cent of guests who first used Airbnb to book a hotel room, and returned to our platform for a second trip, then booked a home'.

Sam Shank, co-founder and CEO of HotelTonight, said: 'We started HotelTonight because we knew people wanted a better way to book an amazing hotel room on-demand, and we are excited to join forces with Airbnb to bring this service to guests around the world. Together, HotelTonight and Airbnb can give guests more choices and the world's best boutique and independent hotels a genuine partner to connect them with those guests.'

At the International Hotel Investment Forum in Berlin in 2019, Airbnb's president of homes Greg Greeley gave more insight into how the platform viewed itself, telling delegates: 'People are going to places that are magical and they're making a connection, they're not having a commoditised travel event.' Magical travel event or not, it looked magically like an OTA.

Expedia Group CEO Mark Okerstrom displayed a touch of the grinchy level-playing fields usually seen from the hotel sector when he told Explore '18[20] that Airbnb had 'raised a fair bit of money from the capital markets and one of the concerns we hear from our lodging partners is that you can

---

[20]www.hotelmanagement.net/own/expedia-conference-takeaway-hotels-should-learn-from-sharing-economy

sometimes get customers to choose something they might not otherwise choose [in the sharing economy] based on price. It's sometimes been subsidised by the capital markets.' Yes, those Airbnb backers were skewing the market and pushing down rates at Airbnb, luring the cost-conscious consumer away. That this was pointed out to hotels by an OTA can only have stuck in the craw.

Back in the mines, Okerstrom continued to push the line that hotels and OTAs needed to work together and that the way to battle this was to use the data that Expedia Group had gathered across its extensive history of transactions. 'I think that gives us an opportunity. We can use information from our flights and lodging stack to make pricing appropriate for hotels and we can get a more-equal playing field with Airbnb.'

Cyril Ranque, president, lodging partner services at Expedia Group, added: 'When it's priced right, when it's not subsidised, the case for booking a vacation rental is more about where people are looking for accommodations for a group of four or more, which doesn't really impact hotel partners as long as we can organise search results in the right way. We have to push more what the customer wants. More alternative accommodations in the rankings doesn't mean fewer customers for the hotels.'

When asked about Airbnb's move into listing hotels, Okerstrom said: 'If you want to have a scale marketplace, you have to have choice, so it makes sense to me that Airbnb is adding this inventory. It's a question as to whether the customer will want it.'

Everyone, Kate Nicholls said, would have to up their game, with Airbnb 'inevitably' moving closer into the OTAs' sphere. She said: 'The OTAs will have to become multidiscipline and Airbnb will logically move into that space. Waitrose[21] does this very well with offerings such as "click here for

---

[21]British supermarket the Queen uses, regularly held up as a How To Do It when it comes to fighting back from online, a remarkable feat considering that it was founded in 1904. And it's a co-operative, so you can't be all bitter about it.

everything you need for Bonfire Night", including products you wouldn't have known about.'

Ramskill felt that, while there was clearly a blurring of lines between the different business models seen at the OTAs and Airbnb, it was likely that the sharing platform would still seek to differentiate itself from the likes of Booking and Expedia, and as such was unlikely to have a significant volume of hotels among its listings.

While the OTAs had been adding peer-to-peer lodging and Airbnb had been adding hotels, Ramskill pointed to those true purveyors of multiple touchpoint travel: the tour operators. The only participants where the customer remains in their hands from airport to holiday and back again, and the only participants, thus far, who have been able to do it at scale, day after day.

At the time of writing, neither TUI nor its rivals had indicated an interest in making Mark Essex's dreams come true and expanding this through-the-journey touchpoint into the corporate market, although if it came with a kids' club there were probably few who would say no.

From such an old and, it must be said, maligned model, could come inspiration and the tour operators, having battled to relaunch themselves online after being outmoded by their online counterparts, had fought back to try to own the consumer from pre-booking to post-holiday and all points in between, in no small part by improving their technology but also by broadening the experiences they offered, from a tour of the local pottery to some flamenco dancing to wash down the warm sangria.

Experiences and being able to book them were the new battleground. Dirk Bakker, CEO at Colliers International, the Netherlands, said: 'I'm afraid that Booking will have to rethink their offering, because they can show experiences quite easily because they have a flexible platform. I'm not sure whether the hotels can do that, because the property management systems they have will need to change to cater for the needs of the travellers, but I'm sure they're going to have to do it. Marriott's got 30 brands, and every one of those brands can offer a different experience.

'You need to be able to express the experience you're offering. I truly think that the way we book rooms is going to change. If you now go into a search engine, you type in the location and from a business point of view that's logical. But if you're on holiday and you're looking for an experience, you don't type in your location, you type in that you want to go hiking, skiing, surfing, then you type in that you want luxury or you want a cabin or you want the beach. People don't like to be bound, they like to be free, to make their own choices.

'At the end of the day, it's experience.'

For Nicholls, there was only one answer and that was to go back to where it all began. She said: 'Hotels need to focus on the service. Hospitality doesn't sell products, we're not retailers, we don't sell commodities – we sell experiences. And if we focus on selling the experience and delivering the experience, then they are the ones who will thrive and survive, so actually they do need to continue marketing, they just need to market in a different way, it's not about shifting beds. I think you'll see it coming full circle and they'll want to take more control of marketing to their own customers. And if we get some controls on the OTAs and if we get some controls on Airbnb, then that will come back into balance.'

Were the OTAs fearful of Airbnb? They were certainly eager to nibble its pie. The OTAs were looking not only at how to take hotel business, but also how to lead the consumer in the ways of devilment and encourage them into the sharing economy.

Expedia Group, which had a dog in the game through HomeAway[22] – which it bought in 2015, having noted which way the land lay – was deeply into the sharing economy and, at the end of 2016, started to integrate its

---

[22] 1.8 million bookable listings at the end of 2018, $11 billion in gross bookings. That's a lot of treehouses.

listings into the main hotels-heavy Expedia brand site, closing 2018 with over 370,000 HomeAway listings on the eponymous platform. A reverse Airbnb, if you will, adding a small amount of sharing to a lot of traditional hotels, while the sharing platform took on hotels. Small beans thus far, but from great beanstalks do they grow. And hotels were already referring to the OTAs as giants.

It was ramping up rapidly. Okerstrom told analysts in its second-quarter call[23] in 2018 that the peer-to-peer lodging brand had added 100,000 new listings in one quarter, commenting: 'Phase two is really about that. It's about international expansion. It's about property acquisition. It's about moving into the urban opportunity. And that's all ahead of us.'

Expedia CFO Alan Pickerill added: 'There is probably no reason that a business like HomeAway couldn't deliver EBITDA margins that look something like the EBITDA margins that you see at a hotel-only OTA.' HomeAway ended the quarter with over 1.7 million online bookable listings, an increase of around 20 per cent from last year. More than 800,000 of them were instantly bookable. Across the wider business, room nights stayed increased 12 per cent while revenue per room night increased 2 per cent. HomeAway saw stayed room nights increase by 35 per cent in the first half. There was growth to enjoy from picking at Airbnb's plate.

It was even prepared to give Airbnb a run for its M&A money, and in 2018 bought Pillow[24], a software solution that helped building owners and managers 'empower their long-term residents to rent their residences', and ApartmentJet, 'a software solution enabling the rental of guest suites in multifamily communities'.

---

[23]https://seekingalpha.com/article/4190963-expedia-group-expe-q2-2018-results-earnings-call-transcript

[24]www.prnewswire.com/news-releases/expedia-group-acquires-pillow-and-apartmentjet-to-enhance-its-alternative-accommodations-marketplace-for-residents-owners-and-managers-in-urban-markets-300737677.html

Okerstrom said at the start of 2019: 'We remain focused on positioning HomeAway and Expedia Group to capitalise on the significant long-term opportunity in the alternative combination space. The goal is really to help customers pick between traditional accommodations and alternative accommodations, and really solve the kind of search and navigation process.'[25]

At metasearch group Trivago, part of the strategy of clawing itself out of what had been a tricky period was to also offer more in the way of 'alternative accommodation'[26]. Rolf Schrömgens, Trivago CEO, told analysts in 2019 that the company felt that the growth of alternative accommodation as a 'substitute for hotels'[27] meant that there was a growing role for aggregators such as itself, which could present both options side by side. If the hotel sector thought that its direct drive was going to overturn the OTAs, it had underestimated how much the OTAs wanted to drive trends – and suck the cash from them. Delicious, juicy trends that saw the distributors present all accommodation as the same, all those heads on a variety of beds, all that lovely commission.

Schrömgens shared an opinion with Bakker as to the future of online distributors, adding: 'I think a trend that we will see in the long run is definitely that we will see that hotel offers will individualise way more than they do today and we see that happening with Airbnb, we see that happening with trends in the industry'.

The loyalty programmes were not just a defence against the OTAs, with whom hotel CEOs were now able to sit on the same panels at conferences without grins looking to rictus. Could they also defend against other threats?

---

[25]https://seekingalpha.com/article/4239277-expedia-group-inc-expe-ceo-mark-okerstrom-q4-2018-results-earnings-call-transcript
[26]They mean someone's flat, not sleeping in a ditch, although that was very hip for a while after being branded as a 'microadventure'.
[27]https://seekingalpha.com/article/4238698-trivago-nv-trvg-ceo-rolf-schromgens-q4-2018-results-earnings-call-transcript?page=10

Estis Green said: 'The loyalty programmes will provide the hotel brands with a moat to protect them against any third parties – today it may be the OTAs but tomorrow it may be Google, Facebook, Alibaba or Airbnb. If you want the end-to-end conveniences and upgrades, or early checkins/ late checkouts or any other things that make the experience easier, better and more friction-free, only the hotel brand can make those things happen because they are controlled within the walls of the hotel. It could be that independent hotels will use the OTAs or other tech firms to provide these services instead of a hotel brand and they will let the tech titans past the front door, but consumers will expect to have that kind of seamless experience. Hotels will have to decide how much to pay for these services and how they will control it so they don't lose control of the customer experience in trying to enable these services within the hotel.'

The battle for the hotel business was destined to come down to that ultimate arena: the hotel itself.

OYO, bitches

Both the hotel brands and the distributors faced a new type of challenger in 2013, with the SoftBank[28]-backed OYO[29] Rooms launching out of India, feeding on the country's position as a global leader in technology, but still a region where the global brands had found it hard to expand. India's reputation was for luxury-beyond-luxury in its hotels, but anything under that level proved difficult to achieve. The UK's Premier Inn pulled out in 2016 after having failed to gain traction and the large globals found that the only way to get into the country was with local partners who could

---

[28]The investor who also bought you WeWork, so may just have something when it comes to disrupting existing industries. Other OYO backers include Lightspeed India, Sequoia Capita, Greenoaks Capital, Hero Enterprise and Huazhu.
[29]Stands for 'On Your Own'. Isn't that, um, hospitable?

negotiate the bureaucracy and local vagaries. Even then, the chance to accelerate through franchises was limited because of the need to maintain brand standards with inexperienced owners.

Enter OYO Rooms, which provided the reassurance of a brand and a route to market for hotels and accommodation providers, bringing with it minimum standards of a like that had not been seen before in India. Through use of its proprietary apps for inventory management, room service, revenue management and customer-relationship management, OYO delivered predictable, affordable and available budget-room accommodation to millions of travellers in India. By 2019, it was also in Malaysia, UAE, Nepal, China and Indonesia.

Guy Parsons, CEO at easyHotel, described the challenge of the Indian market as requiring 'a good partner. The country is enormous and you need to have someone who can unlock the land. It's very different and OYO are attempting, in my view, to tackle a really poor bottom-end market. You have beautiful four- and five-star hotels, then very little mid-market, and then for a lot of working-class Indians they have just horrible accommodation choices and OYO is trying to offer something for that sector.'

In 2018, the platform finalised a funding round led by SoftBank, which valued the budget platform at $4 billion, a few months after Chinese hotel company Huazhu invested $10 million in the group as it expanded into China.

Masayoshi Son, founder, chairman and CEO at SoftBank, used an earnings call[30] to analysts to describe his enthusiasm for OYO, calling it 'a next-generation type of hotel management'. He commented: 'In just two years, it grew the number of rooms in India to 100,000. By the end of the year, I would say 150,000 more rooms or maybe 200,000 rooms, which

---

[30]https://group.softbank/en/corp/irinfo/presentations/

will be 10 times more than Taj group's rooms. It's a completely new type of hotel and they are growing so fast.

'The world's biggest hotel chain [...] is Marriott, and how many net room adds were created by Marriott monthly? It's 8,000. Hilton, the second biggest, 7,000, and it's 2,000 for InterContinental, the third-biggest hotel chain in the world. OYO is not a travel agent. OYO manages hotels comprehensively with OYO's management, with OYO's IT, OYO's booking technology and OYO's quality control method. It's like a franchise.

'OYO helps [owners] to attract people and increase the occupancy of the rooms. So in return for that, the profit will be shared with OYO and hotel owners. And what they do is to create heat maps with AI for demand production. And with AI, they decide pricing. So, per day, 43 million micro-optimisations take place by looking at the weather, looking at the day or week, looking at what kind of campaign is ongoing. Because depending on that kind of situation, demand-and-supply balance is different. So dynamic pricing takes place – 43 million micro-optimisations per day. Without AI, you can't do such micro-optimisation. I believe this is the most advanced hotel management system.'

OYO followed the investment by announcing growth into the UK, its first move outside Asia, using a franchise model to expand, offering redesign, property management and marketing. OYO expanded its model since launching as a platform in 2013, also launching an asset-management arm.

Ritesh Agarwal, founder and CEO of OYO, said: 'The UK has been the topmost international travel destination for several years and last year hosted over 19 million tourists from around the world. Driven by its booming domestic and international travel and budget hospitality needs, the UK presents a multi-billion dollar opportunity for OYO. We are thrilled to now be able to offer OYO's affordable, hassle-free and quality living experiences to guests across the UK – and to be empowering the UK independent hoteliers with the technology and operational expertise that helps them focus on customer experience and thereby generate increased, sustainable incomes.' In this market, which had a strong tradition of branding in the budget sector – no withdrawal here for Premier Inn – the challenges were likely to be greater, but, in a market that has seen independents felled by rising costs and a lack of distribution, there were likely to be pickings from owners considering a last roll of the dice before getting out of the hotel market entirely.

The company said that it expected to be the largest hotel company in the world by 2023.

OYO's success wasn't just based on it being a speedy new platform that branded where no brand has been able to brand before. What set OYO apart was the level of control with which the platform looked at pricing; in this case, 100 per cent control. Owners were told what they were charging, which was unprecedented. This has not been a policy without detractors, though, and The Budget Hotel Association of Mumbai sought to rally hoteliers across the country, telling *The Economic Times*[31]: 'OYO has disrupted the entire market drastically. Rooms that we used to sell for Rs 2,000 to 2,500 are now being sold for Rs 800 to 900. Because of funding, they can sell rooms at much lower rates. The minimum guarantee fee is also not coming, so we are not left with a choice.

'Members from Kolkata, Ahmedabad, Mysore, Bengaluru, Hyderabad and New Delhi have joined us and we will declare the formation of the pan-India association in Mumbai. OYO is not keeping up with the agreements. In some cases, they are telling our members to change the agreements, else they will not pay them, and they are asking for new clauses.'

OYO responded: 'We have always stood for fairness, whether it is to offer quality living spaces at affordable prices to our customers or the

---

[31]https://economictimes.indiatimes.com/industry/services/hotels-/-restaurants/budget-hotels-teaming-up-to-take-legal-route-against-oyo/articleshow/66890345.cms?from=mdr

operational capabilities to help asset owners scale to newer heights by leasing or franchising their asset with OYO. It will be business as usual for us in Mumbai and guest experience will continue to be a priority for us and our asset owners.'

The brands were kicking back. Notably Indian Hotels Company, which has been pushing its Ginger brand. Puneet Chhatwal, MD and CEO at the company, which has its heritage in such luxury offerings as Taj (the chain of luxury hotels owned by the Indian Hotels Company), described Ginger as a great opportunity for the India subcontinent, much larger than brands such as Premier Inn or Travelodge, 'but it has never been executed'. Commenting on the failure of economy brands to gain traction in the past, Chhatwal said that India's consumers were 'more aspirational, they don't want to be identified with anything cheap'.

With 'India's rising middle class' being something of a catchphrase, OYO has sought to expand to feed these aspirational guests, with brand extensions and a move into the business market. To maintain its growth it will need to deal with complaints such as those from The Budget Hotel Association of Mumbai, because, much like the global operators, it is unlikely to move back into ownership any time soon. But until a disruptor comes along to take from its budget core – a level that the globals have no great appetite to compete at – it can have its cake and name its price, too.

Of course this was all too attractive to Airbnb and in 2019 the company paid a rumoured $150 million for a stake in OYO. Airbnb and OYO already shared a connection through Sequoia Capital, which participated in the sharing platform's seed round in 2009, when it had only 1,000 listings, with the investor commenting that: 'They drew us in with their scrappiness, imagination and storytelling – they had a knack for turning a crisis into an opportunity and then a great story. Even then, their commitment to mission, values and culture was clear – and so was their far-reaching vision of a better future by first inventing "a better way to travel", where you are "never a stranger" in a world in which you could "belong anywhere".[32] Sequoia Capital participated in OYO's Series A funding round in 2015.

'Emerging markets like India and China are some of Airbnb's fastest-growing, with our growth increasingly powered by tourism to and from these markets. In many of these markets, OYO is empowering local hospitality entrepreneurs to provide more options to more travellers. We share a dedication to offering people more choices when travelling and we're excited to partner with OYO as we work to make Airbnb for everyone,' said Airbnb's president of homes, Greg Greeley, in a statement.

'Airbnb's strong global footprints and access to local communities will open up new opportunities for OYO Hotels & Homes to strengthen and grow while staying true to our core value proposition. We're excited by the possibilities and committed to bringing benefits to the millions of travellers who can now rely on Airbnb and OYO Hotels & Homes to find a home away from home,' added Maninder Gulati, global chief strategy officer for OYO.

The pair were all about empowering independent hoteliers, or occasional independent hoteliers with this pair, and one's heart swelled with delight at the thought. But what Airbnb needed ahead of its IPO, much as with its purchase of HotelTonight, was diversity and guaranteed rooms. And OYO provided.

---

[32]www.sequoiacap.com/companies/airbnb/

PART FOUR

OPENING THE DOOR – HOW THE HOTELS FOUGHT BACK

Anything you can do, we can't do better

If you can't beat 'em, buy a high-end version of them and expand – that was the response of the hotel sector, with Accor buying Onefinestay in 2016. The platform operated in the realm of aspirational living, at a level many of us could only indulge in by trawling property websites and wondering whether having the swimming pool next to the library represented a damp risk for our first editions.

Kate Nicholls, CEO at UKHospitality, described the platform as not cheap and not for people travelling on a shoestring. But while it wasn't cheap, neither was it profitable, as Accor found when, in 2019, it announced that it was cutting 30 per cent of the properties listed on the platform. Bazin said: 'On Onefinestay we decided to go into the sharing economy, but we decided to go premium, so we have to provide service for that. As an operator I cannot go into Mom and Pop midscale apartments – it would be too cumbersome, too difficult to manage, so we decided to go into the luxury space. There we collect 50 per cent of the rental proceeds and 50 per cent is barely enough for us to make a living. It depends on the inventory. If you have at least 90 days of availability in the same apartment or house, then you get to know the property quite well, the welcomers know how to do the staging – those are fine. What we had accepted too easily were the apartments where we only get the benefit of three days three times a year and this is not enough for us to understand the property and you don't make a living. So we have reduced the inventory to those where we have availability for more than 100 days per year.'

The luxury sharing niche – and Onefinestay in particular – was one area that the hotel sector had, unlike the rest of the sharing economy, chosen not to ignore[1]. In 2014, Hyatt Hotels Corporation[2] participated in a $40 million investment round in Onefinestay[3], only to be bought out by Accor[4] in 2016, when the company paid €148 million, with a further commitment of €64 million to fund international expansion. Always ones to make a point, the deal was the third for Accor in the curated luxury end of the sharing economy that year, having also bought a 49 per cent stake in Squarebreak, which operated a digital platform selling private upscale properties in resort locations, primarily in France, Spain and Morocco, and a 30 per cent stake in Oasis Collections, a curated marketplace for

---

[1] It's worth pointing out that hotel CEOs are expected to stay in properties across their estates. This is slightly higher impact than the CEO of a chocolate company being forced to eat the mass-produced marshmallow fluff every quarter. This is a night's sleep. You're going to want to limit your exposure to the budget sector if you're pulling in a salary of $18.8 million (Chris Nassetta, Hilton, 2017, including stock options) and are used to the finer things.

[2] 182,913 rooms globally at the end of 2017 and brands from Hyatt Centric to Park Hyatt, plus nine others. An active player in M&A, it can usually be relied on to chuck a bid in somewhere and gave us all something to think about in the big NH Hotels Group debacle of 2018, which also gave the sector some fantastic public correspondence and proof that the art of letter writing isn't dead.

[3] They weren't the only ones. Van Paasschen: 'I took a hard look at Onefinestay when I was at Starwood and would have loved to have bought them because I thought they were a very interesting concept and I thought that people who were staying in the kinds of offering that Onefinestay had were the kinds of people that would be part of the SPG loyalty programme.' Busy times in the canteen at Onefinestay, one suspects.

[4] Obviously.

private rentals. Onefinestay featured more than 2,500 homes[5] in London, Paris, Rome, New York, Los Angeles and Miami and they were not cheap – it was not beyond the realms of possibility to pay $1,000 per night.

Despite this – the site split the revenue 50:50 with the owner – Bazin said he did not expect the business to break even until the end of 2019. 'It's actually an investment in expanding the network, opening in new cities, expanding technology, which is absolutely needed to become the world leader,' he said at the time of purchase.

In the event, Accor wrote off a total of €246 million in the summer of 2018 from Onefinestay and concierge brand John Paul after failing to find 'synergies and scaling plans', but it said that 'both serviced private homes and concierge services offer strong potential in the group's ecosystem'. For Accor, the plan was to offer homesharing as part of its hospitality whole, knowing that, for the guest, once tasted, it became a part of their out-of-home retinue.

Marriott International also dipped a toe into homesharing, partnering with Hostmaker, which eagle-eyed readers will recall were working with BNP Paribas on bringing homesharing ever closer to being a real-life asset class. In 2018, the hotel company announced a trial in London, through the group's Tribute Portfolio brand, later expanding it to Paris, Rome and Lisbon.

CEO Arne Sorenson said that it was taking the correct route into the segment, commenting[6]: 'It's one thing for a start-up to engage in a business that really does not comply with law, it's another thing altogether for a 90-year-old company like Marriott to step into a business which is fundamentally illegal. It's a place where branding can make a difference. It's a place where we can deliver an experience both in terms of service and

---

[5]November 2018

[6]https://seekingalpha.com/article/4171861-marriott-international-mar-q1-2018-results-earnings-call-transcript

quality that we want our customers to have. And it's a place where we can feel really good about connecting it to the loyalty programme.

'One of the reasons we didn't jump into this quickly is we thought this is a business that is not made for us. We have now figured out that we can run this business in a way that does fully comply with law. It will include payment of lodging taxes, so that it's a level playing field with the hotel business. It will very much include complying with local regulatory requirements on the number of nights homes can be let in this way and make that work.'

Catty. But Sorenson and Airbnb had history. In 2017, Sorenson told Fortune[7] that the sharing platform was 'spending a lot of money on government affairs and they're playing pretty aggressive. I've had letters from Airbnb directly, demanding my response about some charge, I don't even know what it is, within hours. That's pretty aggressive, and I'm not going to respond to that.'

Airbnb's head of public policy Josh Meltzer then sent a letter to Sorenson[8], asking him to explain to Americans 'your industry's habit of taking billions of dollars from taxpayers to subsidise the construction and operation of your hotels'.

The letter added that Sorenson was 'unwilling and unable to defend your industry's longstanding commitment to price gouging consumers, depressing wages and replacing workers with robots'.

It seems unlikely that Christmas hampers were exchanged that year.

The Hostmaker pilot revealed that travellers were drawn to Tribute Portfolio Homes 'for the curated selection of homes, ease of booking, and service level'[9]. On average, guests stayed more than twice the typical hotel length of stay, sought units with multiple bedrooms and were appreciative

[7]http://fortune.com/2017/11/17/marriott-arne-sorenson-airbnb-moxy-new-york/
[8]www.cnbc.com/2017/11/20/airbnb-wrote-a-letter-to-marriott-claiming-hotel-fleeces-taxpayers.html
[9]https://news.marriott.com/search/all/?s=hostmaker

of features such as full kitchens and in-unit laundries. More than 75 per cent of guests staying at Tribute Portfolio Homes were travelling for leisure with friends and family, or were extending business travel to include their friends and family; overall, the group said, the pilot indicated that Tribute Portfolio Homes resonated with loyalty members.

At the company's security analysts meeting in 2019[10], chief commercial officer Stephanie Linnartz told the audience: 'We realise a premium price for our home rentals and we have growth opportunity in this space. This type of offering does not add meaningful profit, but we believe it will add value to the Bonvoy [loyalty] programme.' Indeed, 85 per cent of guests were members.

Later in 2019 Marriott extended its homesharing product – although not its relationship with Hostmaker – and gained the support of owner Host Hotels & Resorts. Jim Risoleo told analysts: 'We view it positively because it's going to give our existing guests another place to go and to earn points or redeem points as part of the loyalty programme. It will take some pressure off some of our hotels from that perspective. And it should also over time reduce the charge out cost associated with loyalty.

'We spent a fair amount of time looking at this and talking to Marriott about it and the test programme that they ran generated 7,000 room nights from customers who went on the Marriott website to look at a Tribute Home but ended up booking a standard hotel room.

'The properties that they are contemplating putting into this programme are not going to be competitive with us, there is going to be a minimum of three-night stay whereas, our average stay is two nights.'[11]

With owners actively welcoming homesharing – and reporting that it drove business – could the other global operators resist for long?

[10]https://marriott.gcs-web.com/news-releases/news-release-details/marriott-international-announces-three-year-growth-plan
[11]https://seekingalpha.com/article/4259296-host-hotels-and-resorts-inc-hst-ceo-james-risoleo-q1-2019-results-earnings-call-transcript

The 'part of the whole' argument was also being made by the OTAs, who were finding that offering homestays wasn't overly profitable unless you did it at Airbnb's scale. In 2019, Booking Holdings reported that alternative accommodations accounted for approximately 20 per cent of its overall revenue in the previous year. But, as Glenn Fogel, president and CEO, told analysts: 'Sometimes the cost involved can be more than the cost with the traditional hotel product, and it's easier to see that when we start talking about scale. If you want to deal with a hotel that has hundreds of rooms, you can distribute that cost much more easily than when you're going property by property by property. We do very well in the capital cities in the alternative accommodations. We've got great properties there. In other parts of the world, in the US, in particular, we need to increase our properties, particularly single homes in the beach locations … some of the ski locations.'[12]

Indian Hotels Company[13] found a more profitable way to get into homesharing, by looking down the back of the sofa – or in this case, its parent, the Tata Group – and discovering that it had a number of homestay-worthy properties already. The group launched Ama Trails & Stays, a group of heritage bungalows, homestays and guesthouses spread across India, tucking the new brand into its loyalty scheme at the same time. Puneet Chhatwal, MD and CEO, highlighted his own luck, commenting that: 'it just happened as a result of the group chairman's three S strategy: scaling, simplifying and synergising. Because of their heritage, a lot of Tata Group companies have collected guest houses and

---

[12]https://seekingalpha.com/article/4245024-booking-holdings-inc-bkng-ceo-glenn-fogel-q4-2018-results-earnings-call-transcript?page=8

[13]Diversity, thy name is Indian Hotels Company, with a portfolio of hotels, resorts, jungle safaris, palaces, spas and in-flight catering services. The group, founded in 1899, counts some of the world's great luxury hotels in its portfolio as part of its Taj offering, but also includes budget brand Ginger. In total, at the start of 2019, it had five brands and 170 hotels, with a further 25 under development.

homestays over the last 100 years; Tata Coffee in the coffee plantations, Tata Tea in the tea gardens. They are very British, in the Colonial style, which a lot of people love.

'People are seeking a different kind of experience, they don't want to be in a cookie-cutter hotel, they want to go to a spice plantation or somewhere else a little bit different. There is an emerging trend, although it has always been there, for people to travel together; three families might book a bungalow instead of three families going and booking a hotel room. We didn't have to invest, we had these properties available. We can add our operational expertise as well as sales and distribution and branding and marketing, and we think this will help optimise the sales and profitability of the business. We're not adding staff, we're not adding cost. It's optimising the structure we have and utilising it to a higher extent. It is good for our loyalty club, it's something fun for our leisure customers, an alternative to a resort in Goa or Kerala, somewhere people can bring other families with them on their points and have a different kind of experience.'

Hoisting the flag

Fighting in the same territory as Airbnb was fraught. But there was nothing, the hotel sector was inclined to think, that you couldn't fix with another new brand. Owners clamouring to join an operator but the city was full? Give them a new brand so they weren't competing. Owners wanted to join an operator but couldn't afford all the gold and marble? Give them an economy brand. Owners wanting to join an operator but can't be bothered to do any actual branding? Give them a soft brand.

The global operators added more and more brands: to defend against each other with bigger estates and juicier pipelines, to feed their loyalty programmes, to try to create a closed environment where they could be all beds to all people.

Inevitably, almost a decade down the line since Airbnb's launch, the first brand that was unashamedly responding to the sharing economy was revealed: Accor's Jo&Joe[14], a hostel-hotel hybrid offering that started at €25 per night. The group planned to have 50 properties open under the brand by 2020 'in destinations popular with millennials', with city centre sites close to train stations being of particular interest.

Accor worked with UK design company Penson on Jo&Joe – a group that had worked on campuses for Google, YouTube and Jaguar Land Rover but never hotels. Lee Penson, CEO at Penson, explained what Accor was looking for: 'Something holistically game-changing that can't be defined by what we already know and expect. They didn't want a hospitality architect or designer, they wanted someone who hadn't done hospitality ever before. This programme needed an entirely new operational strategy, experience, price and adventurous model. My first pointer to them was to think about "It's NOT A BED".'[15]

And unlike other hostels, this was not a simple rack of bunk beds. The brand wanted to accommodate people travelling alone, in pairs, in groups or as a family, with a variety of different types of room – some, yes, with bunk beds, but some with yurts, hammocks and caravans. There were apartments for up to five people with private bathrooms and kitchen areas. But what the brand placed more emphasis on were the shared areas, with a bar, but also a shared kitchen space.

The brand was also the product of work with Accor's shadow executive committee, a group with, one suspects, a lair, but which was set up by Bazin in 2016 to work on disruptive and innovative projects and address

[14]https://press.accorhotels.group/design-food-ux-accorhotels-revolutionizes-hospitality-with-its-new-brand-jo-and-joe/
[15]https://hotelanalyst.co.uk/2016/11/17/accor-bolsters-boutique/

the challenges faced by trends such as the sharing economy. Composed of 12 Accor employees aged between 25 and 35 years old, Bazin said at the launch of the scheme: 'I can guarantee that 50 per cent of what they'll say will be just the opposite of decisions I'd have taken without listening to their opinion'.

The next year in Davos, Bazin said: 'I only have two women in my Excom. That's why I created a shadow executive committee with 12 millennials: six men and six women. This shadow Excom has the same exact access to information and data as the real one, but the latter won't be able to make any decision that hasn't first been discussed by the former.'

Mövenpick followed Accor's lead and founded a similar committee, a group of 10 millennials, six of whom were company employees, with the remaining four young business leaders. Both Accor and Mövenpick[16] found themselves enmeshed in the latest wave of management: reverse mentoring.

Commenting three years after the launch of Jo&Joe – with shadow Excom still in place, Bazin said that the company had looked at the price challenge posed by Airbnb, but was unable to compete with its existing stable of flags. 'Can I reduce this by 40 per cent? No, which is why we changed our gears, not lowering the pricing of existing hotels, but inventing the Jo&Joe concept, which is not selling a room but selling a bed, and by selling a bed we have reshuffled the floor plan and so all of a sudden you have the same pricing as Airbnb because you have $12 to $15 per bed. Jo&Joe is a pure response to Airbnb.'

The idea of charging per bed not per room was one that had always been washing around the periphery of the hotel sector, but had yet to gain traction. Accor itself had dabbled in hostels with the Base Backpackers

---

[16]In 2018, Accor bought Mövenpick, clearly warmed by a culture so close to its own. Oh and 84 properties primarily in Asia and Europe, with over 20,000 rooms.

brand in Australia, but there wasn't much to fill in the market to tantalise investors until the Generator brand came along in Europe and the combination of pressure from the sharing economy and a move away from the sub-economy 'well, at least it's a roof' ethos of what was a deeply fragmented market. In other words, the potential to bring a lifestyle brand to the hostel sector.

In 2007, Patron Capital acquired the two-strong Generator brand and set about expanding it, leaning on its design-led ethos and strong public spaces. Within eight years, the private equity group increased the property count from two to 11, and in 2017 sold it to Queensgate Investments with an enterprise value of around €450 million, not too shoddy for a collection of bunk beds. However in this case, not just bunk beds, but also private rooms, fast, free WiFi and even meeting rooms. The hostel's business model drove volume and ancillary spend while keeping costs low, and high bed-to-room occupancy rates and low margins and operational costs generated good profits. Investors were particularly drawn to its freehold properties, its flexible build nature and general scaleability of the brand. Show them an old office block in a central location and they saw heads and revenue stacked high.

The branded hostel market has continued to grow, according to figures from Phocuswright, which estimated that by 2020 the hostel market was projected to grow by 7 per cent to 8 per cent year on year, based on a value of $5.2 billion in bed revenue in 2018[17]. In Europe, Savills reported[18] that Berlin was the most well-supplied city and London, Paris and Rome among the least well-supplied. In Berlin, there was a supply of 11.2 beds per 1,000 youth travellers, although this is down from 13.1 beds in 2013 as stock expansion has been outpaced by rising visitor numbers. In terms

---

[17]www.phocuswright.com/Travel-Research/Consumer-Trends/The-Global-Hostel-Marketplace-2016-2020-Second-Edition
[18]www.savills.co.uk/blog/article/240536/commercial-property/millennials-drive-the-hostel-market-to-new-heights.aspx

of growth potential, Savills highlighted London and Paris, as both cities continued to have a very low relative supply of 2.8 and 1.4 beds per 1,000 youth travellers respectively, combined with particularly large numbers of overseas visitors. In the UK, where hostels accounted for just 1.41 per cent of room supply and 0.23 per cent of the active pipeline, there was plenty of room to grow.

While the model worked particularly well in European capitals, where the cost per square foot was high, in markets such as the US, where property and land were cheaper, the hostel market was less successful – you could stick a hotel on the same spot and not have to think about spending money on a pinball machine.

The global hotel operators did not, outside Accor, tend to dabble in the hostels market, but the need to throw another brand at the sharing economy situation remained pressing. Then, in 2018, Hilton launched Motto[19], which it described as an affordable lifestyle brand, offering flexible rooms.

The company said that, having evaluated the emerging lifestyle hostel model, it had found that travellers who stayed in hostels did not like rooming with strangers and often booked just with their friends or family. They wanted more from their hostel experience but were limited by current options in the market. Hilton was there to pick up the slack.

'Following extensive market research that focused on consumers' needs and wants, we discovered the opportunity for a brand that offers travellers a trifecta of centrally located, reasonably priced and less traditional lodging, that provides a one-of-a-kind experience,' said Jon Witter, chief customer officer at Hilton. 'These findings led us to create Motto by Hilton, a flexible environment that allows guests to design their stay, their way.'

---

[19]https://newsroom.hilton.com/corporate/news/hilton-announces-innovative-new-hotel-brand-motto-by-hilton-will-deliver-affordable-style-in-coveted-urban-destinations

The group said that properties would feature 'efficiently designed, adaptable rooms, innovative guest solutions and unique F&B offerings, local to each hotel's respective neighbourhood'. At launch, it had deals in various stages of development in locations including New York City, London, Washington, D.C. and Tokyo, with the company targeting several hundred hotels across all major geographies.

Hilton CEO Chris Nassetta said: 'It's a great product that means we can attract customers who have heretofore not been able to stay with us, and who want to be in an urban environment ... and they need a product at a price point they can afford, whether they are young, in middle age or old. This is where they want to be and this is a product that we are now putting out there that we think will make it much more affordable for them to stay with us. And when they stay with us, we have a pretty good track record of getting them to try other things with us.'[20]

An excellent gateway drug for trying other Hilton brands but not once did Nassetta mention Airbnb, despite Motto also featuring split payments, a product pioneered in the hospitality sector by the sharing platform, where traditional payment offerings largely saw credit cards being swiped at check-in despite already having been inputted at booking. Or Motto including fold-out beds, sliding doors, and private social space. Nope, nothing to see here, definitely no Airbnb competing going on behind these sliding doors.

And for owners? There were concerns about the build cost with such a flexible offering. Tripp McLaughlin, global head, Motto by Hilton, said: 'Motto by Hilton is focused on delivering a more affordable cost-to-build and efficient staffing model for owners. We used a "kit of parts" approach to design the brand – which means each owner will have the flexibility to

[20]https://seekingalpha.com/article/4214030-hilton-worldwide-holdings-hlt-q3-2018-results-earnings-call-transcript?page=13

develop and operate his/her Motto by Hilton in the way that makes most sense for the specific site and market.

'We are working very closely with prospective owners to identify the best destinations and locations. All of our location decisions will center around offering locals and guests an authentic, yet unique, experience. We expect Motto by Hilton properties to be predominantly new build or adaptive reuse projects. We will look at selected conversions, though expect these to be few and far between given the need for micro-sized rooms.

'The development of chain with connecting rooms and the ability to confirm interconnecting rooms at the time of booking is an industry first – and a key feature of Motto. As with all of Hilton's industry-leading developments, we will share best practices and learnings from the connecting rooms with the broader Hilton enterprise, so that other brands can explore and evaluate the feature.'

Accor, mindful of its lost compression nights, sought to take the flexible room offering one step further, with mobile rooms that could be bussed into locations where events met a sudden spike in demand, the sort of spike that sharing hosts had become adept at exploiting. The group launched this temporary hotel concept using shipping containers[21], called Flying Nest[22], after testing it at various cultural, sporting and artistic events throughout France. Sébastien Dupic, new business senior project manager, Accor, said: 'Originally developed for a B2B clientele – event organising agencies, exhibition organisers, festivals, events, corporate clients, Accor partners – the Flying Nest concept could also be offered to a B2C target.'

---

[21]It wasn't the first to look at shipping containers and wonder whether people could sleep in them. Failed UK-based concept Snoozebox spent a few years punting them around F1 tracks before attempting to sell them to councils as residences. If this whole global nomad bit really catches on, presumably one day we will all have our own container to cart around the world with us, like so many snails. But that would destroy the hotel sector, so shh…

[22]https://press.accorhotels.group/accorhotels-launches-a-new-ephemeral-and-mobile-accommodation-concept/

The product used converted marine containers, which are then put into 'islands' of six modules clad with raw and natural materials and featuring a private bathroom, air-conditioned living area and WiFi. The modules of six containers provide five rooms and one 'technical room'. Each island took half a day to assemble.

'The layout of the islands, the patio and the large windows connecting the inside of each room to the outside all provide guests with a totally immersive accommodation option at the heart of the experience,' said Damien Perrot, SVP Design Solutions at Accor. The company said that, through the Flying Nest project, Accor was 'reaffirming its commitment to serving its customers at all levels, including at cultural, sporting and entertainment events'.

Flexibility did not necessarily have to be about the physical product, but about the way in which that product was sold. Airbnb users were used to seeing a full photographic overview of their temporary home in startling detail. Multiple shots of the garden, toilets from every angle, the neighbours caught at work, rest and play. But for potential hotel guests, it was a stock shot of Bedroom Type A. Possibly taken before the recent refurbishment. Or the one before that. There were no options to pick the room or its location. People travelling with groups couldn't guarantee a room together without picking up the phone, and stories were rife of parents who had booked connecting rooms to accommodate their children, only to find the family's rooms were spread across different floors.

GLH Hotels was the first to try to bring choice into the sector, launching Choose Your Own Room[23], a service that allows guests to view, compare and book a specific room within their chosen hotel, which, it said, would put guests in control and end the days of 'making do with the room they get allocated at check-in'.

---

[23]www.glhhotels.com/press/thistle-is-sparing-the-embarrassment-of-causing-a-fuss-with-the-world-s-first-ever-choose-your-own-room-service.html

Features include the ability to view, compare and book the specific room that guests wanted to stay in; a search facility that allowed users to filter results based on location, price and amenities; as well as room layout and even floor plan. Categories include: For Families, For Business, On A Budget, With A View and Suite Stays.

Guest reviews were captured for specific rooms, not just the hotel – so users could also check out what other people had said before they booked. The development of Choose Your Own Room is the next phase in GLH's room booking strategy. The company was the first to offer guests a room selection service – the new service was described as 'a significant evolution, giving even more control, choice and convenience to guests at the point of booking'.

Mike DeNoma, CEO at GLH, said: 'Finally, no more room roulette with our new Choose Your Own Room service. Avoid the booking angst of not knowing what floor, view, layout or size you're getting by seeing multiple pictures of the actual room and even specific room-by-room guest reviews before you book. We've already had great feedback, with 97 per cent of our initial users saying they would use the service again.'

The launch came with a spiffy study[24] that said that four in 10 of us admitted we felt 'anxious' about our hotel room even before we arrived – and one in five couples admitted that poor choice had spoilt their first night away, ending up in a row. If we could, 88 per cent would choose our own room. The company wheeled out behavioural psychologist Jo Hemmings, who said: 'Complaining really isn't in our national psyche, so the anticipation of not liking our room, or even worse, it not meeting our partner's expectations, really can make Britons feel anxious and out of control – particularly when they are outside familiar surroundings and away from home. Airlines have long put us in control before check-in by letting us choose our own seats, so if we are staying the night

---

[24]You have to. Journalists need to see a percentage, even if it's a press release about cake.

somewhere, a system where travellers can really visualise where they'll be waking up is a big move forward which should help combat first-night nerves and help many relax into their trip without being worried about an argument.'

The choice wasn't just intended to bring rapture to guests, prone to fretting or otherwise. It also allowed hotels to practise more effective yield management: they could charge more for the rooftop view, less for the room next to the lift.

GLH launched the offering across 14 of its hotels. The logistical apocalypse likely to be unleashed across, say, Marriott International's 6,500 hotels was the stuff of eyeball-plucking-out nightmare. To retrofit, yes, but InterContinental Hotels Group saw a chance to offer choice when it looked to replace Holidex, its central reservation system, which was launched in 1965[25]. The company started work alongside Amadeus in 2015 and four years later was ready to confirm that its cloud-based Concerto reservation system was starting to offer the ability to pick your own room. Of course, IHG wasn't allowing the OTAs to access this choice – that was for direct bookers only.

The other global operators watched with interest, but also looked to what they already had in their stables that could give the consumer what it was getting elsewhere with the sharing economy: waste not, want not.

Serviced apartments and extended-stay hotels had been starting to creep into the sector, but carried with them an air of road warriors slumped alone on a blocky grey micro-sofa late at night, eating Cup Noodles on their 45th consecutive day of relocating the IT department from Tallahassee to Burlington, and what an unappealing smell that was too.

But the hotel operators could smell cash in those freeze-dried ramen and started waving their brand wands. Staybridge Suites from IHG,

---

[25] And yes, you may well judge hotels, but when was the last time you tried to run a business using technology from the 1960s?

Residence Inn by Marriott, Homewood Suites by Hilton, Adagio by Accor ... housing the wandering traveller became very popular, with markets such as Asia embracing the concept and, after several decades, making up 10 per cent of the total hotel business in the US, albeit it a less glamorous, less talked-about industry segment.

And for once, the emergence of the sharing economy didn't have the existing players running to stick their heads in the sand or to the liquor cabinet. John Wagner, director at Cycas Hospitality, said that on the surface of it, yes, one might think that Airbnb was going to (hush now) kill the hotel sector, but for the segment he was in, serviced apartments, 'my glass half full version is that it's really helping us, because it's introduced that concept of lodging alternatives, providing an apartment, or a hotel room with a kitchen in it, most people had never thought that it existed before, most people never knew, never accepted.'

And one of the key elements with which Airbnb had helped was the acceptance of kitchens. Wagner said that consumers had been unwilling to use serviced apartments because they hadn't seen the point in paying out for a kitchen they would never use. After all, they didn't cook at home, why would they want to cook in another town? But, he said: 'When someone has experienced Airbnb, in an apartment or a house, what they come to realise is that you don't have to cook a big Sunday lunch in the kitchen, but what you can do is you can bring home the unfinished meal from the restaurant or the leftover takeaway, or you can put a six-pack of beers in there. If you're in a hotel for any length of time, it's not about the expense account or the fancy restaurant, sometimes all you want is beans on toast, because, let's face it, nobody eats out for three meals a day all the time forever and it's not a question of money, it's not what you do. You want comfort food, you want casual food, you want a little bit, not a lot, because that's how we eat at home. A hotel room precludes that option.

'When somebody stays in an Airbnb and they have a kitchen, they realise that they don't have to use the kitchen, but they can use the fridge, or heat up a bowl of soup. A hotel room, if you are there for more than a few nights, no matter how nice the room, the rooms just get smaller and smaller and you go crazy. What a serviced apartment does, with the living room, with the kitchen, with the extra furniture, is it's much closer to home than a hotel room is. It gives a degree of mental stability so that you can survive there without going bat crazy.

'And that whole concept of how to live introduces that whole idea to a new set of customers who had never seen it before, because they had only seen hotels. You can stay someplace that isn't a hotel and be comfortable and enjoy it and there are some benefits to that. So Airbnb, for our serviced apartment or all-suite hotel business, is only a positive. I suppose it does take some customers who might otherwise have stayed, but it's far outweighed by those who are introduced to it as a result of Airbnb.

'It expands the universe of travelers, just like the budget airlines expanded the universe of travelers – because prices came down, people who could otherwise not afford to travel, now could. Airbnb did the same thing because their rooms are generally cheaper than hotels – generally – so their guests are, for the most part, people who wouldn't be staying in hotels because they couldn't afford it.'

Despite the rise in telecommuting, the shifting face of the working world has fed workers in through Wagner's doors, with, he said: 'More and more people who are "temporary"; they're contractors, they move around the world doing projects. Historically it was always there – people moved around the world but they worked for a company and their company moved them to a different factory, a different country to import their technical knowledge or their labour in some form. Now it doesn't have to be an aerospace engineer specialising in the ailerons of the F35 jet. Now it can be a regular office worker, but hired on a contract basis.'

Where the sharing economy and the lifestyle segment had an impact on the long-stay market was in the type of product on offer. Wagner pointed to the shift in demand as the leisure sector woke up to the possibilities of a serviced apartment, describing plenty of potential for it in the leisure business. In the US, it was rapidly growing in resort destinations, leisure destinations, 'because it has such appeal for families, especially if you have little kids who don't want to eat out all the time – sometimes they just want a bowl of cereal'.

Investors in regions such as Europe – regions with a workforce often more capable of making it home at the end of the week if not the end of the day because of its geographical size – had, he said, needed educating. 'The overwhelming majority of investors don't understand it, don't believe in it, in many cases are not aware of it. They don't believe in the economics, they don't believe that if you put a kitchen in a room you get a return on investment, they don't believe that there's a case for the return on the investment in the extra square footage in the room against a square box of a hotel room, they don't believe that there's any such thing as an extended stay in their town. That is absolutely not true. I've never seen anywhere in the world where there's no extended stay, and it's growing.'

For Wagner, the reassurance for investors came from using the brands, but also in combining the brands, with properties split into a Residence Inn, for traditional serviced apartment flavour, but also including a Moxy, Marriott International's millennial-focused hotel brand, which looked to offer a boutique, yet budget experience, and, when combined with a service apartment brand, added a dash of colour to a stay that otherwise might be lacking in spirit. A cross-pollination that could well draw in the flitter-flutter Airbnb guest.

The global hotel operators had another option up their sleeve, one that had also been embraced by Asia and one that was so delightful that most of the planet hadn't heard of it and, of those who had, an even smaller number were likely to have used it, much less owned it. For yes, for those with enough cash, you could have your very own branded house. And just when you thought a visible shirt label was too outré.

While a branded residence did not mean a 'Raffles' engraved across every windowpane, it did mean that you could live in the luxury hotel brand of your choosing, while having access to the luxury hotel brand of your choosing right next door and all without the hassle of ownership. You turn up, enjoy it and then, if you had signed a managed agreement, the hotel operator could rent it out for you when you're not there; the very easiest way of owning a second property, although at a cost.

From a developer point of view, if it could be engineered so that you could sell half or a third of the rooms in advance, residences helped with funding or getting cash back and you could make some profits. The brand in this case added a verifiable premium, with Graham Associates[26] putting that premium at around 20 per cent to 30 per cent.

Savills World Research estimated that there were more than 400 branded residential schemes globally, with a combined stock of approximately 55,000 residential units. Hotel brands were the dominant force and accounted for some 85 per cent of schemes. Marriott International was the largest single player with a market share of 31 per cent among hoteliers by number of schemes. But the largest individual brand by number of schemes was not a hotelier, but Yoo, a brand built on design credentials, with more than 50 branded schemes in operation.

Paul Tostevin, associate director, Savills World Research, said: 'New brands will give hoteliers a run for their money. Tech companies, already disrupting the car industry, may be a natural fit. Luxury food and drink brands may be another contender.'[27]

---

[26]https://howtospendit.ft.com/house-garden/203036-branded-residences-upping-the-ante
[27]www.savills.co.uk/research_articles/229130/267029-0/the-future-of-branded-residences

There was even a convenient by-product: for standalone residences, cities such as Barcelona – which had a moratorium on hotel development and on the sharing economy – had no such restrictions on anything that could be used as housing, monogrammed or otherwise.

So successful was Marriott International finding it, that when it announced that its branded residential portfolio was expected to grow by more than 70 per cent in four years from 2018[28], it also said that, while by 2022, about 70 per cent of the company's branded residential properties were expected to involve one of Marriott International's luxury brands, the remainder of the pipeline featured premium, non-luxury brands such as Marriott Hotels, Sheraton, Westin and Autograph Collection.

Tony Capuano, EVP and global CDO at Marriott International, said: 'As the number of residential condominium buyers grows globally, Marriott International's well-known brands are ready to welcome them "home" and deliver a distinct experience. We are excited to work with world-class developers to help them deliver highly desirable and successful branded residences to market.

'Residential developers know that we are not just involved with creating a beautiful luxury residential project with a compelling list of amenities and services. We're also laser focused on creating dynamic communities where people can enjoy a convenient lifestyle and personalise their experiences – just as they do in our hotels, which is why Marriott International expects growth in this segment to continue.'

Dynamic communities, being welcomed home, convenient lifestyles? It all smacked more of home than of hotel, more of Airbnb than Marriott International. The difference was in the community: one real, one manufactured.

---

[28]http://news.marriott.com/2018/09/marriott-international-plans-to-expand-its-branded-residential-portfolio-by-more-than-70-percent-by-2022/

The C word: community

Airbnb, more than its competitors, has sold itself on community. Live there. Live like a local. Even if it did not always deliver – and even if the locals you were living with cast malevolent gazes in your direction – it was a potent message, speaking to a society in which living alone, disconnected in person if connected by technology, was the norm. And social shifts aside, it was reacting to the hotel sector, which had evolved to separate itself from the communities in which it set up shop.

With the exception of destinations such as Miami Beach, where passes to hang by the pool were the norm, the local population had not been encouraged to come into hotels and the hotels have not looked further outside than the tassels on their doormen's uniforms. The big brands sought to reassure the nomadic businessman, as Guy Parsons, easyHotel CEO noted: you wanted to be able to navigate a Novotel wherever you were in the world, even if you couldn't speak the language.

Technology has helped to change how we work the world. We aren't quite at *The Hitchhiker's Guide to the Galaxy* levels of being able to stick a babel fish into our ears and understand everything said around us, but Google means that we have a good idea of what our destination will look like before we get there, where the local bus stop is, and there is a strong chance we can buy the bus ticket online before we are even in the same country. With great knowledge comes great desire for more once we get there. It isn't enough just to know what the road looks like, now we want to get more involved, to know that we went to the most authentic restaurant, danced at the bar the locals dance in, went blind from the same bucket-distilled hooch. And yes, social media has encouraged our appetites for showing off, but there is a deeper thrill to be had from the feeling that you went somewhere and, just for a day or two, could guess how it might feel to live there, too, rather than just surviving it from within your branded bubble.

The isolation of hotels had gone a long way to informing the opinion of governments around the world that the sector didn't matter, that it was providing services for foreigners, offering a smattering of low-level jobs that, really, no one wanted, and would just about do for the locals until they got real careers. It had done a great job of making itself invisible and yet, in 2016, travel and tourism generated $7.6 trillion, 10.2 per cent of global GDP, as well as accounting for 313 million jobs around the world, equivalent to one in 10 jobs in the global economy. The sector made up 6.6 per cent of total global exports and almost 30 per cent of total global service exports, according to the World Travel and Tourism Council[29].

The success with which hotels were able to vanish while being in plain sight in their communities meant that, while such numbers never failed to get a reaction when they were revealed, it was rare that they were aired at all and rarer still that governments took account of them when considering policy, or were moved to consult with the sector when making decisions. One of the few regions that sought to base an economy around the travel and tourism sector was Dubai, which, with an empire based on rapidly-draining oil reserves, realised it had to look elsewhere. So it launched Dubai 2020[30], with the target of attracting 20 million visitors per year by 2020, doubling the number received in 2012, with the target extended to 23 million to 25 million visitors a year by 2025. Tourism, the emirate said, would be the central tenet of its economy.

---

[29]www.wttc.org/economic-impact/
[30]Of course, all the hotels piled in and the oversupply was ruinous for rates, but never mind. It's all about the long game.

This enthusiasm for travel, tourism and hotels meant that the local response to them has also shifted in Dubai, with Lennert de Jong, commercial director at citizenM, seeing a destination where 'most of the community spend their time in hotels. The best beach access is in the hotels; there you see integration into the community, even if the community is 90 per cent expats. But you see that in some countries where the hotels are bringing the standards, where they are better than local restaurants. But if you go to the main Western cities, it's an illusion'.

While travel was booming, hotels were failing to deliver a product that felt like travel at all. Frits van Paasschen, author, citizenM advisory board, former Starwood Hotels & Resorts president and CEO, identified the shift, with stakes having changed, and a quiet, clean room now being taken as read. What was increasingly scarce, he said, was a sense of place, 'the feeling that I'm going somewhere and I'm getting an authentic experience. I know that we've used to death words like "authenticity" and "curated" but they mean something. And what they mean is that people search for "Wow, I stayed in someone's house near Venice Beach and I got a feel for what it's like to live that life", not "I'm staying in some tall building somewhere and I have to get a cab to go to the beach and it's not fun by the time I get there".'

This, for van Paasschen, was what Airbnb had achieved, the idea of bringing people back to a sense of place, 'even with the idiosyncrasies, [it] has created something that's changed the expectation of travellers, whether they're staying in a hotel or non-traditional lodging'.

Those putting up the boxes were hearing the call for change. Architect Dexter Moren, founding director at Dexter Moren Associates, who practised across the UK and Africa, said: 'Why are you going to Paris or why are you going to Amsterdam? People don't want the standard room that they find all over the world, they want something that is embedded in what's local. Millennials are looking for experiences, and if they want to come to a city, they don't want to be isolated in a hotel, they want to know what's going on. There has been a fundamental change. It used to be that hotels were a secure place where only the guests were allowed in, but hotels aren't like that any more.' More and more, he said, there was an interface with the street, which is where hotels were going.

Moren had seen this shift for the past decade, as the slow-moving beast that is the hotel sector started to feel the prickle of changing demand and, as an architect, Moren was looking for ways to deliver it. Hotels he said, had started to exist as part of a community and, for him, Accor were at the forefront of embracing this. 'A decade ago, Accor's motif was that, wherever you were in the world, a Novotel room is a Novotel room. Sébastien Bazin's attitude now is that wherever you are in the world, he wants you to wake up and know which city you're in, know which location you're in. It's a key change'.

'You walk into an Ibis and honestly, you wouldn't think it was a hotel. You walk into a brasserie. The barista will take you in, where there are a few people with some iPads who will check you in. Reception doesn't exist and that for me is what hotels are doing. They are full of people on the ground floor who are not staying upstairs and it's invigorating. You don't want somewhere with a bunch of seats like a furniture showroom, you want life.

'It's exciting – Sébastien Bazin has said that he doesn't want to see any receptions. The old property adage used to be "location, location, location". For hotels, it's now "local, local, local". Local in the sense of attracting locals, it's local in the sense of its design and it's not design for London, it's specific for that location. So if you go to a hotel like the Bankside Hilton [in London] it's absolutely related to where it is, it is a totally different feel to doing a Hilton in, say, [spiffy location] Mayfair. We try to embrace it in terms of its location, we try to embrace it in terms of its facilities – so that it attracts people from the street who aren't staying there. The big thing is food and everything is local provenance. We've got hives on the roof and they have their own honey – and that's the way it's going.'

That food, bees or no, would offer hotels a chance to be part of the community and to offer more than the OTAs could, and certainly much more than Airbnb, by creating something where people actually wanted to be when conscious. Not so much of a revolution, you might think, but an area where the hotel sector had fallen behind since Don Draper was propping up the bar, as anyone who has enjoyed a meal with no one but the waiter for company could attest. Efforts were made to create branded restaurants for branded hotels but the guest was unwilling to eat the same food around the world before returning to their identical rooms and, without wishing to tar to excess, the world's greatest chefs were not lining up to open a restaurant in a hotel, where the clientele were always on the move and were unlikely to come back every Wednesday for the crab.

This, as anyone calculating revenue per square foot against revenue per room was inclined to note, was a money-wasting error. No wonder people were looking to put yoga into dead space. It also, as Marieke Dessauvagie, hotel consultant at Colliers International, pointed out, failed to take into account people's lazy inclinations, because, after all, what could be better than staying in a hotel that has a good restaurant, 'then you can take the elevator upstairs and roll into your bed. It brings an extra vibe to the hotel – it's a place where you want to be, it's a place that you want to be part of. The F&B part of a trip is becoming more and more important for guests, and hotels should make more of an effort. As long as you have a good concept, people will come'.

Nicholls agreed, describing Soho House as 'particularly good at that: where you're looking at exploiting the F&B offer and working the dead space. It's fairly rare that people eat in the hotel that they're staying in, they want to go out instead, and eating in your hotel had such a bad reputation. It's about going back to the traditional coaching inn, hotels in the centre of market towns, where they think first and foremost about F&B for the people who are walking around and the rooms are an extra. That's a mindset that more hoteliers need to get into. It's a more authentic experience and what you're talking about there is a personal experience.'

The Great Northern Hotel in Kings Cross, London, was betting its business on the importance of getting F&B right – not just for its guests, but for those who were passing and felt a certain parching of the throat. Owner Jeremy Robson said that it went 'to the heart of our offer. We try to run our F&B outlets as if they are independent businesses, not ancillary to rooms. We have F&B specialists who have all worked in top-end successful restaurants; not restaurants which are a tertiary element to the rooms, because hoteliers generally do not make good restaurateurs. They don't bring best practice into the particular use – be that a martini bar or a restaurant – and what I wanted to create were destinations for each of our offers and then for the hotel guests to have the benefit of these destination F&B offers.

'It's a core element of our offer and it means that we should get a premium to the average daily rate. Our food has a Michelin-starred chef director[31] and our food is produced by one of London's best destination restaurants [Plum and Spilt Milk[32]]. Our breakfasts are incredibly good and cooked to order off a cleverly conceived menu. It's not a buffet, which is what a hotelier would probably want to do.

---

[31]Mark Sergeant, who spent many a year being shouted at by Gordon Ramsay. See? Shouting works. Don't tell HR.

[32]Taking its name from the distinctive livery worn by the dining cars, the Flying Scotsman first pulled out of King's Cross. Not Farrow & Ball.

'If you come here, it's a halo product. Car manufacturers often have a special product into which they invest heavily, to get the benefit across the rest of the range, and that's the philosophy I have. I would never run a hotel without the benefit of other elements to my business. Restaurants are operationally geared, so you have a lot of fixed costs, and you have to work incredibly hard to make a profit, especially at high end. It's risky, but the nature of this business is that people come with high expectations, which means that the real challenge for us is to maintain and consistently hit those best standards. I do it because it aids the rooms business, which is more efficient in terms of profit, but also it fits the location, because I have 128 million people using this transport hub. And if you're a resident, you might be more comfortable dining in the hotel restaurant because you won't see it as a hotel restaurant. Boutique hotels tend to get away with that more than branded hotels and when you have a celebrity chef like we do, there is an allure, an attraction to staying in to dine, if you create the sense of an independent business.

'The corporate hotel market brings a standardisation of service, a reassurance and lots of good things – loyalty programmes[33] – but when it comes to high-end dining and drinking, I think it's important to have a sense of that soul and independence and spirit. If you've been trained in the big corporates, you can be a highly professional manager and there's that consistency and assurance, but as an owner and as a guest I don't want that to come through. I want professionals who come from a more esoteric and individual spectrum who work to exacting standards.'

Robson said that around 98 per cent of the hotel's F&B revenue came from non-residents, with 50 per cent of the hotel's total revenue coming

---

[33]And he would know – the Great Northern was a member of Marriott International's Tribute Portfolio – branding lite.

from F&B. So it made sense to keep an outward focus at the property and counter the feeling among many communities that hotels had just been parachuted in. To this, he felt a strong sense of the hotel's place, adding: 'I want to be part of the community, that's a really important thing to us. There's a duty you have – we're a big business in many ways, it's a high-profile business and you want to be part of the community. We're rooted.'

Bringing the surrounding neighbourhood inside was also embraced by Moren and his team – they built one hotel whose design echoed a Maasai tribesman – but it was the interiors that attracted the community. He said: 'We coined a phrase called "neighbourhood story" many years ago with the Ampersand [in London] and shortly after that everybody wanted a neighbourhood story. Everything about the Ampersand's interiors was inspired by its location: by the V&A, by the Brompton Oratory ... those themes came through, they were inculcated into the whole project. That's how we design buildings. Architecturally, we would look at what fits into a location – sometimes you want to create something which doesn't fit, which is iconic, but usually urban context is something where you want a good-quality building in context and sometimes planners are more adventurous. From an architectural point of view, we are trying to design something which has some emotional response to the peculiarities of a site.'

Accor decided that they wanted to go further than the bricks and mortar and, in 2017, launched AccorLocal, an application allowing residents who live near an Accor property to access 'the services of local artisans and companies' as well as the hotel's amenities.

Services included: flowers delivered to the hotel's reception, with AccorLocal's special bouquets in collaboration with Pampa, Bergamotte and others; yoga, Pilates and relaxation classes provided by Oly Be, and held in a room let by the hotel; quality bread delivered by Poilâne;

pick-up and deposit points for Nespresso capsules that were accessible 24/7; and a pay-by-the-hour AccorLocal car rental service, offered by Hertz 24/7.

Launching the project, Bazin said: 'For the past 50 years, millions of customers around the world have trusted Accor's hospitality expertise. When they go through the door of one of our hotels, they can be certain of finding, at any time of day, a customised service offered by more than 250,000 people who are passionate about our unique *savoir faire* in the field of hospitality and service. We have now chosen to make this unparalleled wealth available for the benefit of community life by developing an unprecedented model, creating social connections and value for small businesses, local communities and staff members at our hotels.

'We need to diversify outside of hotels. We will continue to work in hotels for the next 50 years, as we have over the last 50 years, but what about when our colleagues want something more? What about when some people want more than just a hotel room?'

Bazin divided Accor into three verticals: the core hotel business, the travel business outside traditional hotels, and 'community services', the latter of which he said would have 'nothing to do with travel but it's plugged into community services. But the three have something in common and it's very important: it's customer relationships. The database will be common to the three. The loyalty programme will be common to all three. Technology will be common because the three will mutually enrich each other.' Done right, he said, verticals two and three would represent 30 per cent of mid-term results within five years.

Scott Gordon, AccorLocal's CEO, said: 'Today, the problem we have is that we only see our customers a couple of times a year. Our ambition is to be recognised as your daily life companion, not just your travel companion. We've been focusing for the past 50 years on the travellers of the world and had forgotten about the local community, which is five or six times the size. After all, who else is open 24/7, other than the police, hospitals and hotels?'

Two years later and Bazin said that the initiative had gone too far, too fast and 'in too many directions. It was difficult for the users to understand. We are refocusing into megacities – Paris, Barcelona, Amsterdam – we are mainly looking at helping people with their lives. You want help with babysitters, you want help with having food prepared; we are trying to do it much more niche, much more specialised. But it is going to take much more time than we had expected for the local community, who had previously been barred from entry, to understand it. The guy next door has been told for the last 20 years that it's not for him. But we are getting there. I am still shouting that this is a good idea, and once we have proven services then we will expand. Some work, some don't work. But I'm a pretty impatient guy, I come from private equity, so as much as I think it is a good idea I need it to work.

'If you are going to be using space, you need that space to be paid for. If you are only going to be selling bread I can add five cents to the price of a baguette – I need to sell an awful lot of baguettes to make a living. What works well is the neighbourhood using our spa, which is unused from nine in the morning until seven in the evening, and we bring in yoga classes using social networks and they pay $10 for using the space and that is good for us.'

A similar service was under trial at 25hours Hotels, in which Accor was a shareholder and where bread and yoga were also features. Christoph Hoffmann, 25hours Hotels' CEO and co-founder, said: 'We are becoming a bit more analogue when everything has become a bit too digital. Our hotel group is not five star but we think that people appreciate good advice. We want to offer services to our friends, to our neighbours – we offer rolls and baguettes to our neighbours before they get up, it's easy for us – we already have the rolls.'

There was no additional charge for the services, with Hoffmann commenting: 'It's not something that pays off directly. We have to have interesting people, we have to pay for the technology, it all costs and we are asked how does it pay off, when do we get our money back? We know people appreciate it, but we don't want to ask for fees. But I think we can add value for the guest. When you check in it's about passports and credit cards, not interesting things. If you have someone who takes away that pain, it's a much better experience.'

Accor had sparked a trend, as Moren found after working on one of the first Hotel Indigos for a demanding InterContinental Hotels Group. 'They said it wasn't what they wanted, so we redid the public areas with entrances on the road to the bar and deli and this was then the F&B offering for the hotel, but also for the locals and it all means that the hotel becomes a more dynamic place,' he said.

Hoffmann acknowledged that integrating the hotels back into the community[34] through extra service was 'not there yet, we don't have masses of people coming to the hotel, it's a learning process. It's a question of how you communicate it. But I'm very confident that it's the right thing to do.'

For James Bland, director at BVA BDRC, returning hotels to where they once were, in the centre of a community, 'is a laudable aim, it's part of the thinking at Accor. People are looking for something which is authentic and what could be more authentic than that?'.

You can, of course, go too far in terms of community interaction, with de Jong, like Bazin, eyeing the bottom line. 'The last time I checked, as a hotel you provide amenities to attract guests and to keep them happy at

---

[34]And yes, that does conjure up an image of halfway houses, but then haven't hotels committed crimes against hospitality?

the rate they are paying. The last thing you want is to bring in all kinds of locals; I understand that you need to be a good neighbour and not have rooftop parties that keep everyone awake, but I wonder what purpose it serves unless you are a really F&B-driven outlet. For us, the majority of our revenue is from rooms and what we do extra must generate a profit or it should enhance guest satisfaction in a way that they are willing to pay more for.' In other words, come on in, but not if you're going to nurse a latte all day and hog the WiFi.

For citizenM, and a growing number of hotels, the answer to this was to embrace the co-working trend. After all, it can't all be about bread and yoga; the local community has to work to pay for your fabulous services and why not let them work under your roof. Who knows, they might stay and buy a sandwich or drown their sorrows in the bar after a trying conference call. It's not all about giving back, there's money in those with whom you share a neighbourhood, money which Airbnb was also eager to snaffle as it tried to move deeper into the corporate market, partnering with WeWork as well as offering properties on its platform for business meetings.

In 2013, Marriott International launched Workspace on Demand[35], a collaboration between it and LiquidSpace, a mobile/web app connecting people in search of flexible workspaces with venues providing workspaces, which the operator said would be 'easy to find and simple to reserve, just like a hotel room'.

Paul Cahill, brand VP at Marriott Hotels, said: 'We are challenging the notion that you have to be a hotel guest to use the hotel. We are opening the doors and saying, "Come in, work in our lobbies and use our free WiFi. Gather your team in our meeting rooms, whether it is all day or just for an hour." We made the process easy and are giving our customers the ability to book on whatever device they prefer.'

---

[35]https://blog.liquidspace.com/marriott-expands-workspace-on-demand-powered-by-liquidspace-program-to-more-hotels/

Marriott International's plans to relaunch its Sheraton brand went in heavy on co-working, with a special table featuring lockable drawers and a raised platform for not knocking your coffee on to your neighbour's laptop, a feature that used to entertain many a sector hack at that time. And it worked – the table showed up in *Architectural Digest* as part of a feature on chic co-working spaces.

Accor entered the sector in 2017 through a joint venture with Bouygues Immobilier, formed with the aim of accelerating the growth of Nextdoor in France and Europe, having identified that within five years, flexible workspaces could represent 10–20 per cent of office space in France, compared with 2 per cent at the time. Two years later, Bazin reported that Nextdoor was the second-largest co-working brand in France, with over 50,000sq m (538,000sq ft) in 12 locations, running at 92 per cent occupancy, but acknowledged that 'at the pace WeWork grows, we will never make anything out of it if we can't scale it up'.

Tom Carroll, head of EMEA corporate research at JLL, said that co-working was something that had been around for a quite a while, but was evolving quickly 'and impacting on the real estate sector in its widest sense. We've seen an impact on the real estate sector and on individual workplaces, as organisations large and small embrace greater flexibility, but we've also seen an impact on the hotel sector. At its core, co-working reflects a fundamental change in how individuals are working, driven by technology and the mobility that that provides. We are seeing different requirements and preferences from the workforce and that's across all age segments. We're also seeing the growth of the SMEs and the gig economy, and all these trends are creating new and different types of requirements of workspace. One of the ways that is playing out is the increase in flexible office space and the growth of co-working.'

His colleague Jessica Jahns, head of EMEA hotels and hospitality research at JLL, said that, from a hotels perspective, a number of hotels were looking to transform underused spaces, such as the communal areas and outdated business centres, and were looking at co-working as a way to generate additional revenue. She said: 'Some hotels have great lobbies but are often underutilised and could be used better. There are opportunities on quiet weekday mornings and other quiet periods when spaces could be converted into co-working areas.'

Jahns pointed to examples of hotels which have charged for the space, for example with a 10-day co-working pass. The Hotel Schani in Vienna offered a 10-day pass which works out at around $100 and which allowed people to hire the space. In London, there was a company called Spacemize, which operated almost as a third party, with exclusive partnerships with some of London's luxury hotels, including the W and the Andaz. In addition to having access to WiFi, and tea and coffee, members also had access to discounted rates on food and at the bar.

'There haven't been brands within brands at the hotels themselves. The TryTryp by Wyndham in Dubai has a co-working space which they have branded Nest. Apart from that example, I am not aware of any other specific co-working brands specifically focused on hotels'.

Carroll said: 'One of the things with co-working is that it is still early days, there is a lot of experimentation and different providers are looking at different ways of providing the space, curating the space, aligning it with different offers for clients or members. There is a lot of diversity and the creation of a more vibrant community is widely reported to be a potential benefit of the spaces themselves. The classic open co-working space is a one factor which drives some of the positive engagement you hear from the users. The co-working providers themselves curate that community: they have community managers, they run events, they have a diverse F&B offer, and so on. In some ways, the wider co-working market borrowed a lot from the wider hospitality industry, and in that sense the hotel sector is well placed to provide some of these services. We expect continued diversity in terms of adoption, as there is no single driver here: some are looking to monetise directly, some will be looking at creating additional communities and taking a club-like approach, some will be looking at the success of Soho House and others.'

But were hotels building a hardworking community or just providing space to rest a laptop? Were they going far enough in their consideration of road warriors and, just, well, warriors who worked from home. Even before WeLive was a twinkle in WeWork's eye, Hans Meyer, one of the founders at citizenM, launched Zoku in Amsterdam – an office-cum-serviced apartment hybrid that, it said, aimed to combine the services of a hotel with the social buzz of a thriving neighbourhood. So far, so on trend, but the product also included Community Managers, tasked with making professional connections and introductions in the city, something many would be more than happy to outsource. The product included office space in the apartment, but also co-working space for those moments when you wanted to stare at a human while having deep thoughts about quarterly returns, as opposed to staring at a blank wall. 'The interesting thing about extended stay is that it is quite difficult to make it work in the city centre,' said Meyer. 'What we focus on is giving global nomads a social life'.

The general population was on the loose, escaping cube farms and roaming the world, looking for the locals, looking for somewhere to work, somewhere to eat something other than a club sandwich. But what was all this doing to brand standards? A branded hotel company with brands twitching and flexing with every consumer trend was surely one where the brands themselves became less and less distinct?

This, said Moren, was not the case. The brand standards, he said, would be in terms of some of the spatial arrangements, 'but once you move up the food chain, the brand standards are a lot more flexible. Overall, if you have a hotel with X number of keys, they'll want to have those sorts of facilities. They're more flexible at the top end than at the bottom end and they're all going this way. The Hilton we did at Bankside in London is a core brand Hilton. One of the major hotel brands turned it down because of its location on the South Bank – who went to the South Bank 10 years ago? – and when it opened I took them to visit and they said: "But this is not a Hilton". And I said: "That's exactly the point".

The sector was moving closer and closer to being less about identical block hotels and more – despite van Paasschen's lack of passion for an overused word – about experience.

The in-body, out-of-room experience

The former Starwood CEO wasn't the only one to be wary around the concept of 'experience'. After all, said director at collaborative marketing communications agency THC/Endeavour, Imran Hussain, 'Why are we talking about experience all the time – we all have them every day?'

'What we want,' he clarified, 'are great experiences, and great experiences are not cheap. This industry is run on standardisation, but you need to look at your asset in a different way, you need to look at what can happen within it, whether it's talks, seminars, events or dog shows, because it has to happen within the building for the hotel to market itself as a place of experience.' And looking at experience through the eye of the money-maker was critical, with Dirk Bakker, CEO, Colliers International, the Netherlands stating: 'Five years ago, the best institutional hotel product to invest in was Holiday Inn Express. Today, it's not even in the top 10. Why? Because Holiday Inn Express does not offer an experience.'

Hotels were good at delivering once-in-a-lifetime experiences, as Robin Sheppard, chairman of Bespoke Hotels, attested – they were adept at serving a purpose, such as enabling you to propose marriage to the person you love. But, with a few exceptions, that's not a weekly occurrence and if it were, it would be likely to dull somewhat, no matter how spectacular.

The efforts by the global operators had led to experiences becoming a required aspect to loyalty programmes, but these experiences largely took place away from the hotel and backstage at a concert, or watching the Accor scheme versus the Marriott scheme on a football pitch, for fans of post-modernism.

As anyone who has gazed at a PowerPoint in a windowless room at a hotel conference over the past decade can attest, 'experience' was one of those things that we all needed to enable others to have and then riches would surely follow, be that day-to-day or in dog-show form. Transferring this from concept to reality was something of a head scratcher, but that was only to be expected given that the 'experience economy' was a term emanating out of Harvard back in 1998, not a location renowned for its hospitality degrees.

In a paper by B. Joseph Pine II and James H. Gilmore[36], the experience economy was described using the TV show *Taxi*[37] in which Iggy: 'a usually atrocious – but fun-loving – cab driver, decided to become the best taxi driver in the world. He served sandwiches and drinks, conducted tours of the city, and even sang Frank Sinatra tunes. By engaging passengers in a way that turned an ordinary cab ride into a memorable event, Iggy created something else entirely – a distinct economic offering. The experience of riding in his cab was more valuable to his customers than the service of being transported by the cab – and in the TV show, at least, Iggy's customers happily responded by giving bigger tips. By asking

[36]https://hbr.org/1998/07/welcome-to-the-experience-economy
[37]As opposed to the film *Taxi Driver*, although we've all stayed in that hotel at one point or another. Stayed, if not slept.

to go around the block again, one patron even paid more for poorer service just to prolong his enjoyment. The service Iggy provided – taxi transportation – was simply the stage for the experience that he was really selling.'

An experience, the pair said, occurred when a company intentionally used services as the stage, and goods as props, to engage individual customers in a way that created a memorable event. This did not, hoteliers would be relieved to note, mean that everyone had to go all Planet Hollywood and burst into song every hour on the hour.

Sheppard added: 'The customer wants experiences and so anyone who says: "I have just the hidden coffee shop for you that no one else will tell you about", is precisely what they are looking for. The hoteliers are going to be saying, "I don't want to tell you about anything outside my hotel, because I want you to spend all your cash in my building." There is no incentive to tell you about anything that might be nearby and will take you away from where you stay.

'So as I see it, as the generations go by, the Airbnb approach and mentality of thought and anticipation will become increasingly important. There will always be a demand for a fabulous culinary and bedroom design experience. You want to feel pampered, you want to feel that the quality of the fixtures and furnishings is to a style that you really appreciate, that you feel it's better than your home by some distance. I don't think that will go away. But experience is more.'

The experience of the taxi passenger was more linked to what the brand represented, how well this could be delivered and how memorable it was. As our Harvard authors noted, the easiest way to turn a service into an experience was to provide poor service – thus creating a memorable encounter of the unpleasant kind. They elaborated: 'Overservicing in the name of customer intimacy can also ruin an experience. Airline pilots interrupt customers who are reading, talking, or napping to announce,

"Toledo is off to the right side of the aircraft". At hotels, front-desk personnel interrupt face-to-face conversations with guests to field telephone calls. In the guestrooms, service reminders clutter end tables, dressers, and desktops. (Hide them away and housekeeping will replace these annoyances the next morning.) Eliminating negative cues – by transmitting pilots' offhand announcements through headsets instead of speakers, by assigning off-stage personnel to answer phones, and by placing guest information on an interactive television channel – creates a more pleasurable customer experience.'

With intangible words such as 'experience' floating around the sector, more were bound to follow, and the relaunch of the Ibis brand introduced us all to the concept of the 'life hub', which was, the brand assured us, what a hotel now was. The hotel was now a venue 'where anyone can come to sleep, dine, meet people or enjoy live music'.

For de Jong, it didn't have to be the experience itself that was on site, but that the hotel had helped to facilitate it. What Airbnb was doing with its experience platform, he said, was 'raising the bar on the service that it provides. If you look at a typical hotel, what service does it provide? There's a concierge who gets paid by all the restaurants they recommend – he's your gate into that unknown city – then there's room service, or housekeeping service. If you can order from Deliveroo at the gate at Schiphol airport, why would you ever bother with the service that hotels provide?

'What Airbnb has done on experiences is going to disrupt and hotels need to respond. If it's just a place to sleep for a night, that's OK, that doesn't matter. If there are all these extra services, then hotels just need to facilitate it – why not? Why do you need to cook in your own hotel? If you have external parties that can do it better, then why are you not helping your guests by curating those services from outside?' The experience for the guest was one of getting what they wanted, in as easily and friction-free a way as possible. No need for Planet Hollywood here.

But who is delivering this new experience?

Being a consumer in the real world wasn't fun any more. The same brands along the same streets, with automatons behind the desks who have no real power or authority to add zest to your day in case they fall foul of training manual B, subsection 48, paragraph 12. You might as well stay at home and order the same thing online and if that jumper is the wrong size, well, never mind, DHL will come and take it away. This is a great shame for anyone who grew up watching *Sex and the City* and being sold on the idea that shopping was a fun day out, drinking champagne at Manolo Blahnik. To be fair to the world's luxury shoe sellers, that still is fun. But for those of us not spending $800 on a pair of shoes, the consumer experience leaves much to be desired. The convenience of online has stripped us of experience.

Mark Essex, director, public policy at KPMG, was prepared to come out and say so. He didn't like shopping, it made his feet hurt and it cost too much in expensive coffees that you had to buy along the way. He elaborated: 'I think that choice is hassle and consumers don't want choice. And I can prove it. If choice was the chemical of human existence, how come you never see Rihanna browsing all the choices in the supermarket? What she does is she has a personal chef and she tells that chef what she likes and that chef goes out and browses the shelves on her behalf. It's just a job, but a job we perform for free because supermarkets persuade us it's something we enjoy. It's the same with shopping, it's supposed to be a leisure experience, but no one does it any more because we realised it's not that much fun. What you want is what you want when you want it. And if you had a personal stylist who sat you down in a chair and brought all the dresses to you, that's the experience you want: you do the choosing for us and you recommend.'

Barry Sternlicht, CEO at Starwood Capital[38] described good customer services as being 'how to not fail your customer'. In other words, getting the basics right. So quoted Yotel founder and CEO Gerard Greene anyway, and given that Starwood Capital invested $250 million into Yotel in 2017[39], it's likely that this came with a side of pithy management advice.

Customer service and staffing have become the bête noire of the hospitality sector. It's the primary point of concern and one where it stands the most chance of competing with the sharing economy and winning. Airbnb made much of the role played by hosts in helping their guests achieve the local life and have the authentic experience, but this is somewhere that hotels also had expertise, even if they had allowed it to become buried.

But it was easy enough for Airbnb: their hosts – at least the ones who it liked to talk about in its marketing – lived onsite, or very near. They came with the property and didn't cost anything, either, which was the kind of daydream that in which most GMs, indeed most CEOs, didn't allow themselves to indulge, even after a whole wheel of cheese. And that growth in travel, which was helping to keep the impact of the sharing economy at bay? Well, more demand for more hotels meant more people to staff them. In 2017, the WTTC said that travel and tourism accounted for 313 million jobs, or one in 10 jobs around the world[40]. That did not include the number of vacancies.

---

[38]And chairman of Starwood Property Trust and co-founder of Starwood Hotels & Resorts. See 'Sternlicht', think 'Starwood'.

[39]www.yotel.com/en/discover/press/news/yotel-announces-partnership-with-starwood-capital-group

[40]WTTC, Travel and Tourism Economic Impact 2018

Efforts to get around it were made, of course. In 2015, a Japanese company leapt into the breach and offered up a hotel where guests were served by robots, and a series of jokes questioning the difference between the technology and the computer-says-no attitude of some check-in staff was born. Four years later and the Henn na Hotel in Japan announced plans to cut its robotic workforce by more than half and return to the human option, after a series of complaints from both guests and staff – the latter because they had to keep working overtime when the robots broke down. Nothing too out of the ordinary there, but some of the failings were ones you would hope to avoid in the human world.

In one case, the in-room robot kept waking a guest up to get clarity on what it thought were questions, but were in fact just rambunctious snores. The same robot would also attempt to join in conversations between guests, in a trying fashion. Another issue became apparent when robot luggage carriers were unable to access any rooms without perfectly flat floors. The whole thing was far from ideal.

One way in which to avoid having to hire robots was to create brands where staffing was limited, a trend that was to be found at the budget end of the spectrum, where keeping rates at an attractive level for guests meant hotels uncluttered with staff. Frits van Paasschen described the growth of hybrid lodging as 'not quite like Airbnb was conceived, more like a hotel such as we've come to know them. Staffless, no F&B, all-suite hotels like Sonder[41], can compete very well without the labour costs in high-cost environments. This is a space that will become important.'

---

[41]'The consistency and service of a great hotel that doesn't come in a typical hotel format, combined with the warmth and comfort of staying in a space that feels more like a home', says Sonder, which, had 16 sites at the start of 2019.

The Scandinavians had a head start on this, as Peter Haaber, the founder and CEO of Zleep Hotels[42], noted, with his successes in making a profit in the region with an economy brand. He said: 'Labour costs here are extremely high – we pay a housekeeper €20 per hour, so we need to be more efficient. You need fewer people here because we have a flatter management style and people are taught to take responsibility. If you look at the social models of Scandinavia, we can cut out a lot of middle management and give opportunities to the workers instead.'[43] HR teams, head to Scandinavia now.

Globally, the staffing shortage varied across different regions, but a broad brush identified Western markets as suffering the most, because they had a high volume of hotels and a high volume of citizens who didn't want to work in them. 'Hair or care', as an aged relative said to this author about where one might send an idiot niece, the inference being that not much of an intellect was required for either. Not exactly an incentive. Other issues, apart from slurs from relatives, included not great pay, terrible hours and a perception that if you start as a dishwasher, that's where you'll stay.

In the US, the Bureau of Labor Statistics estimated an annualised employee turnover rate of 73.8 per cent[44] in the hotel and motel industry. Most headhunters would tell you that 10 per cent was a better rate and that 10 per cent marked a culling of the less productive; this was the kind of turnover that you needed to make yourself a more effective organisation.

The issue in many of the mature markets was that students didn't look into their tax-paying future and swoon at the thought of serving others, a problem that particularly affected the UK. Robin

---

[42]With nine hotels in Denmark, the brand was set for expansion after Deutsche Hospitality bought a 51 per cent stake in 2019.

[43]*Hotel Analyst*, 4 February 2019

[44]Including restaurants, which included seasonal staff on their rosters.

Sheppard, chairman at Bespoke Hotels, said that this came with some compensations – that it kept payroll low – but for anyone looking to sell their hotel on the basis of its fantastic service, as he was, this was a bittersweet saving. For Bespoke, staffing issues began with the difficulty of hiring chefs, which Sheppard said had seen the group give up trying to appoint permanent chefs and focusing on appointing permanent agency chefs instead. And try getting one of them to work on Christmas Day...

For more general hotel staff, Sheppard said that the group had been working with colleges in South Africa, Sri Lanka and Italy. He said: 'There isn't an imaginary pool of labour [in the UK] which says "great, I want to work in hospitality". And if you want to have great service in a hotel, you have no choice but to employ Italians. If you say to any child leaving school in the UK: "There's a restaurant or there's a cafeteria, where would you rather work?" The child would say "cafeteria", because British staff love clearing dirty trays from a table and not engaging in eye contact with other people who have just been sitting there. Whereas an Italian will come to the table and chat with that customer, pour the water while they're talking to them and feel entirely at home. We are hardwired not to serve, for some reason.'

For Sheppard and other hoteliers in the UK, Brexit was to stymie his route into hiring Italians, along with the other European workers who had helped to staff the rapid expansion in the service sector that the country had seen, particularly in restaurants.

He added: 'Sadly the view is: "Oh, you're in hotels, are you? Did you have dyslexia as a child and you can only do practical stuff? Or you're a cerebral creature? Oh, you can't possibly work in hotels then." I think Tony Blair has a lot to answer for[45], when he drove so many into

---

[45]Sheppard was not the only person in the UK to have a list of things they felt Tony Blair might be to blame for.

university education, because the concept of getting into a business, working your way up, learning, it's not a bad idea.' As Bazin had noted when launching AccorLocal, the need to centre a hotel in its community was key to its success, something Sheppard agreed with, commenting: 'GMs of hotels, if they want to carve out their niche, need to be a de facto mayor of the local town. They need to host a lot of events, they need to speak at a lot of meetings, they need to be a personality – that's old-fashioned hotel-keeping and I don't think they have been teaching that as well as they could.'

Even if willing students could be found to populate the hotel schools, they might not then work in hotels once they graduated. Chris Mumford, founder of Aethos Consulting, said: 'People who've been to hotel school don't want to work in operations because it's hard work, they don't want to work at the weekend, they don't want to work at night, and their friend who was in the same class at university is doing a nice 8.30am to 6.30pm job in consultancy, flying around the world.

'And then you see other sectors compete for that talent. The Swiss hotel schools have seen the Swiss banks come in and take their people, because they have the hospitality and service skill set, so you put them into private banks in customer relationship roles and it's great. Do you work for a Swiss bank or do you go and work as an assistant room service manager for 18 months and then maybe move on?'[46]

Assuming you could find staff at all, Nicholls said that hotels needed to make sure that they met all the needs of customers. 'What hoteliers need to do,' she said, 'is to understand their market and who they are approaching. It's about keeping pace with changing customer demand. You can give your guests an authentic experience, because what they are looking for are the top tips, or where to go to have the experience in

---

[46] The Brexit Report 2017: from uncertainty to opportunity

that city that a native has. If you look at some of the research that's done around London, international tourists coming to the city want to go out in the parts that Londoners go to, that's what's partly fuelling the interest in some parts of the city – but they don't know where to go. The illusion that Airbnb gives is "come and stay in Shoreditch, and you'll have more of an authentic experience", which is why the top hotels still attract the best customers, because they can tell you where the hottest place is to eat. The one that, if you google "top restaurants in London", might not show up. Smaller, independent hoteliers, can look at recreating that experience.'

Nicholls looked to such smaller independent hoteliers to lead the drive into offering a more useful concierge service than that identified by de Jong. She did not call for the large branded operators to forge a path, unintentionally pointing to one of the issues facing the global hotel companies: with so many interested parties at each site, who were employees loyal to? With a hotel potentially having an owner, a franchisor, a third-party operator and a brand, were you working for Hilton? Or were you working for the owner? Or the person whose name was on your paycheck, which could just as easily be a third-party operator? Hotel brands had distanced themselves from their guests, but also from their employees.

Sheppard said: 'If you're part of a company which is obsessed with central purchasing, you're never going to get to know the people who can do local jobs for you. If you work in a local hotel, it's mandatory that you have to have a day when all the taxi drivers come into breakfast and you tell them about your hotel and the price positioning and what the main facilities are and you give them a little incentive to keep recommending.'

Bazin was quick to shoulder the blame, describing Accor and many other companies as being 'so draconian in numbers of standards, codes of conduct – tying your hand behind your back. We have a couple of hundred markers which you have to follow because they are the markers of the brand. And probably half of the clients are either upset with it or they don't want to see it any more.'

Parsons was one of those budget operators who focused limited staff on key areas, which in easyHotel's case was recognising regular customers and helpings guests to do that which they'd come to do, whether that was visiting the theatre or seeing a local tourist attraction. He was also a hotel guest who would recognise Bazin's assertion that consumers wanted a different variety of service, commenting: 'I'm not disabled yet, I can take my luggage to my room, but if you find you have to take it, please let it get to the room before I do'.

As van Paasschen said, hotels were all Don Draper in the bar, combined with ideas of what travel was 40 years ago. Bazin said: 'The way to break it and the easiest way – which is a dangerous one, an audacious one, but which works superbly – is that you have to hire people from outside the hotel industry. You hire artists, you hire anyone with a good heart, with good common sense and you can create superb hoteliers. We train them a bit, but there is nothing better for a client than to have somebody rendering the service who looks like him.' And this, said Bazin, was why tattoos were no longer forbidden.

Mumford agreed with Bazin, commenting that: 'To be a successful hotel company you need a balance of people from within the hotel sector and outside it. I'd like to see more people from the hotel sector get snapped up by other industry sectors, but at the moment it's very much a one-way street, for some reason. When was the last time you heard of a hotel CFO going to a drinks company? The hotel industry has come a long way in the last 10 years in terms of looking outside its borders; in terms of functions such as marketing and HR there are disciplines where you can bring people in from other sectors.

'The old days of having to take bags up to the room and work in the kitchen before you can work in the hotel sector are over.'

For Accor, it wasn't just about allowing tattoos; the company looked to completely overhaul its training and address the issues that came with having a global company. Bazin had already taken care of the 'who reports to whom' issue: 'The GM reports to us and has a legal relationship with the owner, but in 100 per cent of cases, all of the GM's hires have to join Accor Academy. Because of this they feel they are working for Accor – which no one minds, everyone is pretty pleased with it. And for me, the DNA of them being associated with Accor is a big benefit.'

In 2016, as part of efforts to bring the group's 'Feel Welcome' ethos to life, it launched a product called 'Heartist'. Bazin explained: 'We did a survey in 40 countries asking: "What do you think you guys have in common?" across different brands, different cultures, different education. What was it that they had in common? Of course they said Accor.'

Of course. But, said Bazin, 'what came out was exceptional, what I would have dreamed – in different jurisdictions they came up with the associations of two things: heart – generosity, you do something without thinking, as if it is natural – and "ist" as in "artist", because you have been trained. Now we have the Heartist programme and whether you are in France or Nigeria or Korea they will talk about Heartist and it's the new common denominator wherever you are, or whoever you are.'

So taken was Bazin with 'Heartist' that he said he considered renaming Accor as Heartist. He didn't. 'I've been trying to battle over the past years to make my brands very much associated with Accor. Accor as an employer name means nothing, because it's not B to C. Clients don't care about Accor, they just want to go to a Novotel or Pullman, so if you rename

Accor as Heartist that's several hundred million spent on a brand, which is probably better spent on a commercial brand.'

And he was right. Then in 2019, at the same time he was convincing no one that the group had stepped back from its M&A frenzy, Bazin said that he would be focusing 99.9 per cent of his time 'on what matters most: team, brands, loyalty and guests. I want to retain those key people who were leaving, because they want more mobility. It is too much cost to lose 50,000 people a year. There is a great effort to be made in giving them additional education.'

The value of additional training was not lost on Will Hawkley[47], global head of leisure and hospitality at KPMG, who said that yes, companies that offered training, opportunities and benefits were more likely to keep their staff – and may find it was more efficient to have better-skilled staff who stay. But he also forecast that he expected to see more companies coming up with benefits, 'such as one high-profile coffee chain's offer of interest-free loans for house deposits'.[48]

At Accor brand 25hours Hotel, Hoffmann was working to ensure that, as the brand expanded, it would not fall into the cookie-cutter traps of its global peers. If you want to keep your soul, he said, you needed a Soul Manager, which, he explained, ensured 'that we are trying to keep our philosophy, to make sure that the tribe will be extended to that place. They take care of different things: the emotional aspects of a hotel, how do you feel the hotel when you enter it, what's the kind of atmosphere, what's the kind of music, what's the attitude which you experience as a guest when you come into the hotel. We cannot dictate out of Hamburg

---

[47]Regular viewers of BBC soap opera *EastEnders* will note a small appearance by a police officer named Will Hawkley, named for the KPMG leisure advisor.

[48]Widely rumoured to be Whitbread. Of course it went on to sell its Costa Coffee brand to Coca-Cola, so now you'd have to ask them. https://home.kpmg/uk/en/home/insights/2017/08/the-brexit-column-no-time-for-leisure.html

or Zurich how people behave in Singapore or Melbourne. We can already feel it when we go to our properties in Vienna versus Berlin; even in this little region there are different types of culture and you have to give a certain freedom. But you need a common denominator to keep the brand alive and once you have it, we can hopefully control it in a way that's not going to be lost.'

For Hoffmann, 'You cannot do anything on a centralised basis any more if you are big. You can distribute some information on a centralised basis, but you have to empower the hotels more and more. You have to make sure that the GM, the key personnel, people who we choose to create the tribe and the philosophy of 25Hours ... we make sure that we are closely connected with those people. Bear in mind that the kind of contracts that any brand has internationally includes the fact that employees are not employed by the operator, they're employed by the owner if you have a management agreement, or if you have a franchise it's even stronger. Not being close to your employees is a challenge. Since we have more than 1,000 employees, a lot of outsourced people, we try to educate via a "train a trainer" concept. We focus on a lot of people in our hotels who [in turn] become ... the people who help to make sure that new people who come are trained the right way – it's not done centrally.

'If you have a type of hotel which offers quite a lot of experience, and have F&B and public spaces and certain service amenities, you can compete with Airbnb, but if you are a hotel which doesn't have a lot of features or experiences, it is harder.'

Accor was also looking to take a step back from micromanaging in its M&A activity. In 2014, the group bought a 35 per cent stake in boutique brand Mama Shelter, which was created by the Trigano family, who helped build the Club Med concept, with support from Michel Reybier and design collaboration from Philippe Starck. The company combined accommodation with a strong food and beverage offering, which delivered 65 per cent of revenues, and, while Accor was expected to help the brand expand[49], Bazin said the decision to only take a one-third interest was based on preventing Mama Shelter's innovative ideas from being watered down. 'The minute we're integrating too much into their system, we may defeat those fresh eyes that they have, which is part of their success.'

This practice was then repeated at 25hours Hotels (30 per cent), 21c Museum Hotels (85 per cent), SBE Entertainment (50 per cent), Mantis Group (50 per cent), Nextdoor (50 per cent), and Banyan Tree (5 per cent). As Bazin said, Accor's employees had spread all over the globe, launched brands and then came back to the group when they looked for growth. He, meanwhile, looked to his 50-brand target.

In addition to trying to avoid issuing decrees from above, Hoffmann took the non-traditional hospitality route of focusing not on the guests, but on the employees[50] because, he said, the group was struggling 'like everyone else, to find good people, even to find enough people – we have an overall lack of headcount in the kitchen, for example. The industry is struggling – how do we train, how do we teach a culture not only from the guest point of view but from an employee point of view?

'It took me some time to understand that guest orientation cannot be everything. Back in the 1990s, the thing was that the guest was everything. But who was our customer, was it the guest or the employee? As long as the employee is not delivering the quality of service at reception, at housekeeping, in room service, or on the face-to-face contact points, you will always lose. The focus has to be on the employee, not on the guest. If you focus on the employee, the guest will profit from it. That detour is very important and many hoteliers, including myself, haven't appreciated

---

[49]And did, to 12 sites by the beginning of 2019.
[50]There was no word on whether they too were always right.

it. But it's not done by rules or regulations any more. It's done by behaviour, it's done by an attitude: giving people the empowerment to act individually, to act in ways so you don't have to tell them everything they have to do in a certain situation. You cannot tell everybody everything in every situation and that's why you have to give trust, to give them a very good education.'

Hoffmann, like many others, was hoping to lean on technology to improve the lot of guests and employees alike and had high hopes of a bright new tomorrow. He said: 'I'm sure we'll have so many things to offer in the future that will change the guest experience. It might be labour, or that digitisation will take over some of the check-in and check-out procedures, particularly for budget hotels. If you go to a lifestyle or luxury hotel, it may be completely different: digitisation supports employees to offer additional or different types of service. If you don't need to have a check-in or check-out any more, why not use the employee to offer a more profound, more interesting service? You can change a lot of the experience for the guest and also for the employee because they don't need to focus on targets, they can focus more on quality.'

Hilton sought to combine technology with the knowledge of its staff by adding a feature to its Honors rewards programme app[51], which included staff recommendations, on food, nightlife, shopping and activities, curated[52] to appeal to a variety of audiences.

'In listening to our guests, there is a real desire for more personalised travel advice and access to local perspectives surrounding best restaurants, attractions and neighbourhoods to explore,' said Joshua Sloser, senior vice president of digital at Hilton. 'No one knows their city better than local Team Members, which is why we're empowering them, through Hilton

---

[51] https://newsroom.hilton.com/hiltonhonors/news/hilton-introduces-explore-a-new-local-travel-feature-within-the-awardwinning-hilton-honors-app-powered-by-foursquare
[52] Inevitably.

Explore, to provide the latest local recommendations to enhance our guests' experiences.'

There was bound to be conflict between man and machine, and it wasn't always destined to go the way of man, as was proven in *Terminator* – and they had the help of time travel too. Marriott International's attempts to make digital assistant Alexa take the strain hit a fleshy lump when members of the Unite Here union voted to strike over the implementation of the technology, which they feared would start to take away jobs. Unite Here's president, D. Taylor, said: 'You are not going to stop technology. The question is whether workers will be partners in its deployment or bystanders that get run over by it.'[53]

For a sector that had so far been largely immune to technology taking its jobs, there was concern that robots were going to do what they had done to the automotive industry. A 2017 report from McKinsey Global Institute, *Jobs Lost, Jobs Gained: Workforce Transitions in a Time of Automation*[54], estimated that technology would drive a 30 per cent decline in jobs in food service and lodging from 2016 to 2030, with an eye on jobs involving customer interaction.

It wasn't just McKinsey. All the consultants were making money with disturbing reports into how the robots were taking over. PwC's *Will robots steal our jobs?*[55] was a little more chipper, warning against believing in 'the Luddite fallacy' that there would be a terrible impact on jobs, preferring to point to long-term benefits (although it did warn that 25.5 per cent of accommodation and food service jobs in the UK could be at risk) such as

[53]https://unitehere.org/newsroom/

[54]www.mckinsey.com/~/media/mckinsey/featured per cent20insights/future per cent20of per cent 20organizations/what per cent20the per cent20future per cent20of per cent20work per cent20will per cent20mean per cent20for per cent20jobs per cent20skills per cent20and per cent20wages/mgi-jobs-lost-jobs-gained-report-december-6-2017.ashx

[55]https://webcache.googleusercontent.com/search?q=cache:0bYLoKqdp6IJ:https://www.pwc.co.uk/economic-services/ukeo/pwcukeo-section-4-automation-march-2017-v2.pdf+&cd=4&hl=en&ct=clnk&gl=uk

general growth in the economy, which would feed through to spending on services where, for the foreseeable future, robots 'may not be able to totally replace, as opposed to complement and enhance, workers with the human touch'.

It mused: 'While traditional machines, including fixed location industrial robots, replaced our muscles (and those of other animals like horses and oxen), these new smart machines have the potential to replace our minds and to move around freely in the world driven by a combination of advanced sensors, GPS tracking systems and deep learning, if not now then probably within the next decade or two. Will this just have the same effects as past technological leaps – short-term disruption more than offset by long-term economic gains – or is this something more fundamental in terms of taking humans out of the loop, not just in manufacturing and routine service sector jobs but more broadly across the economy?'

And those routine service sector jobs that so few people wanted to take up? There was hope yet that robots might come to the rescue after all and bring a more positive view of the industry to potential job seekers, once the grind was taken out.

Bazin was already aware of the rolling in of digital disruption, but felt that it was more likely to have an impact on his distribution rivals, commenting that a bigger disruptor than Airbnb was 'clearly a combination of artificial intelligence and the Internet of things. You could have sensors in your hotel rooms, the ability to design the lights, open the windows, put your content on the TV. All that is disruption and we have to be tech savvy.

'AI will increase even further the demands of our clients. Google Home or Amazon Echo are a pure demonstration that those devices in your home know you by heart within six months. They know the way you talk to your children, they know the way talk to your husband, they know if you talk about having any financial problems because they have heard you talking to your bankers. They know if you are sick, if you are in a happy mood or a silly mood. They are likely to disrupt the OTAs – you will see Amazon and Google interfering with recommendations. Because your children are unhappy, because you have financial problems and you're stressed, that device will tell you "Sorry to interrupt your discussion, but there's a big sale on holidays in Brittany for next weekend and I know you have problems, but your family needs a break. Your bankers won't know about it".

At citizenM, de Jong described AI as 'a bridge too far – we are not there yet'. But the company used smart learning to provide answers to guest queries, with the machine aiding the human – rather than the other way round – and helping to respond when it detected that a similar question had been answered before, such as driving directions to a particular hotel. He pointed to the advantages that smaller groups of hotels had over large global players: 'Independent hotels,' he said, 'are in a much better position to gather data – you can learn a lot when a guest stays three or five days with you.'

Where it was hoped that technology would help out in delivering decent customer service – but without antagonising staff, ruining careers and bankrupting the masses behind the backs of their bankers – was by trawling that immense amount of data that hotels had gathered on their guests, in no small part using their ever-swelling loyalty programmes.

The personal touch

Hotels sat on a lot of data. Really, an absolute stack. Sometimes they sat on it; sometimes, as one hotel did, they chucked it unshredded into a skip behind the hotel for anyone to come along and lift all the credit card details (but since GDPR that isn't supposed to happen any longer). Mark Okerstrom and his colleagues at Expedia Group made much of the data they had stored and understood how useful it could be to hotels, but the hotels themselves had it within their power to use it just fine on their own – if only they could just unlock it.

For Frits van Paasschen, this data itself was enough to motivate the consolidation in the technology sector that saw Marriott International combine with his former shop, Starwood Hotels & Resorts, if, as he described, 'you started to think of hotel companies as technology platforms, designed to create a way to deliver personalised hospitality to high-end travellers around the world'. He added: 'The larger the system, the more money you have to amortise over a bigger system and invest in that technology. The flipside of that is you have a huge system, with these legacy systems behind them and, as much as scale can be an advantage, it can also be challenging. There's a big transition that all the large hotel companies have to make before they become agile and before they can take advantage of that scale.'

A transition that Marriott International found very challenging indeed when the Starwood Hotels & Resorts database found itself breached. But it all ended well and, once shored up, a personalisation machine could be created.

A study by the GBTA[56] found that 84 per cent of business travellers said that having a personalised guest experience was important to them and, importantly to hotels, 80 per cent of the guests were comfortable with hotels using shared information to provide a personalised guest experience. And what did they want? Primarily special offers – the devils! – but also restaurant and entertainment suggestions.

---

[56]www.hotel-online.com/press_releases/release/gbta-research-reveals-business-travelers-say-loyalty-matters-in-hotel-booki

'From booking to check-out, our research confirms personalisation is highly valuable to business travellers, with many seeking customised hotel experiences that are tailored to fit their business travel needs,' said Jessica Collison, GBTA director of research. 'Both travel buyers and suppliers should evaluate how personalisation factors into hotel booking and the guest experience when it comes to building their travel and loyalty programmes.'

You can go wrong, of course. One enterprising hotel chain, which shall remain nameless to save its blushes and the chances of being named in any divorce cases, thought it would be jolly nice if it put a photo of the road warrior's family up on the room's TV screen, for a little home-from-home comfort. As they discovered, it's best to check whether said warrior is shacking up alone or has a guest in tow – a guest who might not expect such a level of personalisation or increased knowledge of their paramour's family tree.

But horrific, life-changing personalisation aside, there was also money to be made from tailoring the hotel experience, with Boston Consulting Group observing that brands that created personalised experiences by integrating data and advanced technologies were achieving revenue increases of between 6 per cent and 10 per cent[57]. Personalisation was vital, the company added, because consumers have caught up to the digital age and expect to be able to tailor their own online experience. Customers want their experience to be situationally specific to them and they have learned this from Airbnb and the OTAs, but also from their experience on the streets.

The group pointed to Starbucks, a vendor of coffee but, since 2014, a source of interactive games, which it sends to loyalty programme members through email and its mobile app. The games provide a fun way to reward

---

[57]www.bcg.com/en-gb/publications/2017/retail-marketing-sales-profiting-personalization.aspx

loyalists and motivate them to try new products and visit stores more often. Since 2016, the games have been personalised – one customer at a time, using data gathered from past visits and digital interactions.

The consultant described it as 'a smart move and a profitable way to engage customers with the brand. The personalised games have helped to triple Starbucks's marketing campaign results, double email redemptions, and generate a threefold increase in the incremental spending of customers who redeem offers. The results come with increased marketing effectiveness, enabling Starbucks to reduce its mass-marketing spending and invest more-personalised marketing dollars with the right customers, thus incentivising the right behaviours. But Starbucks has bigger plans: it is developing one-on-one relationships at scale. It is individualising its brand by giving each customer his or her own personalised experience that encompasses in-store visits, digital interactions, and even, potentially, products offered.' Personalisation was more than just writing your name on your cup.

In the UK, John Lewis announced plans to invest £400–500 million a year to differentiate the business through products, customer service and services, many of them driven by technology.

Suzy Ross, senior retail strategist at Accenture said: 'With consumer expectations sky high and brand loyalty plummeting, consumers are crying out for retailers to change from the sellers of "stuff" to the givers of great experiences. And only some are listening. It is encouraging to see the partnership pledging a highly personalised, experiential retail service which could achieve the differentiation needed for survival. For retailers like John Lewis to really thrive and deliver experiences that will keep customers coming back, they must embrace new technologies to rapidly respond to changes in consumer behaviour and harness data, insight and artificial intelligence to anticipate and personalise individual customer interactions.'

Hotels didn't have to make a meal of it when it came to using data – unless it was a meal the guest had requested, liked before and wasn't allergic to. It didn't have to be hard – to paraphrase McGyver, you could please your guest with data that you already had lying around from previous stays, including length of stay, average amount spent, popular room type requested and purpose of stay. As Frits van Paasschen said, one simple way to make your guest feel appreciated was to know that when they are travelling alone and for less than a day, maybe don't upgrade them to a suite they won't appreciate and in which they won't enjoy spending half their stay switching the lights on and off.

Partnerships played a part in this personalised ecosystem. A Deloitte study into GX[58] – guest experience – reported that guests could order a rideshare quickly, order food delivery from local restaurants, and schedule a fitness class on their phones in seconds, so hotels should be making it easy for guests to engage with their preferred vendors. This partnership ecosystem had benefits for all types of hotels, as it helped them to provide the experience guests want while reducing hotels' total cost to serve.

Deloitte noted that, whether a hotel was in the luxury, full-service, select-service or lifestyle tier, most did a good job in meeting travellers' basic needs, with 79 per cent of those surveyed satisfied with these elements. There would always be opportunities to deliver incremental value on the basics, but clean, well-kept rooms in safe locations at a good value are expectations, not differentiators. Hotels represent these elements as the basics. These were the critical factors a hotel must have in order to earn a hotel guest's stay. They are not typically the notable factors cited by guests that led to an exceptional experience, though they are high in importance.

---

[58]www2.deloitte.com/us/en/pages/consumer-business/articles/hotel-guest-experience-strategy.html

Over the last few decades, hotels have been able to differentiate with sustainable practices, notable facilities, amenities or signature products, public spaces, and food and beverage. Now, many guests often expect the availability of such things. We represent these elements as the new basics because they have shifted from experiential differentiators to core expectations, meaning their absence and/or a subpar perception of them may negatively impact the stay more than their presence and a positive perception of them will create an exceptional experience. The opportunity to differentiate exists beyond the basics and the new basics. It is widely acknowledged, inside the industry and beyond, that engaging guests meaningfully and creating lasting, positive impressions is the path to obtaining and retaining guest loyalty and advocacy. But with guest expectations higher than ever and previous 'differentiators' now serving as the cost of entry, how can hotels continue to elevate their game?

The message was getting through, with both Marriott International and Accor relaunching their loyalty programmes with a view to being able to recognise the guest when they walked through the door and to do something for them that proved that they were a person and not just a collection of points with a tier on top. Loyalty could be used not only in the battle for business from the OTAs but also, to look back at the Cold War, the battle for hearts and minds. The hotel sector is based on personal connections. It should be able to make them count.

As with so many of the innovations that hotels are only just starting to look into with purpose, personalisation was something that was always possible, but that the sector needed a kick to embrace. A healthy shove in the right direction.

Personalisation, van Paasschen said, was 'a combination of things, one of which is literally personalised service. Technology and scale can offer ways to do that better than a traditional innkeeper might have done years ago just by being a good hotelier. The combination of that kind of recognition and a good understanding of what individual preferences are is something that could and should be implemented systematically across hotel systems, and it's absolutely a way that the larger hotel chains should be able to compete. It's just taking them a very long time to get there.'

Conclusion

Having my son opened my eyes to new experiences, gave me fresh insight into the world and all that parent-book stuff, but even more importantly, jabbed me with the realisation that the hospitality industry was dominated by cookie-cutter hotels that wanted all their guests to form the same shape. And if you didn't fit, you could forget the shiny copper bar with the 50 brands of whisky and signed portrait of Hemingway, because you, fee-paying guest, were drinking in the corridor, or in the bathroom, or in the dark.

Was peer-to-peer lodging a disruptor that bought the hotel sector closer to seeing the light? It certainly gave it the yips for a while and held up a mirror to an industry that had become too satisfied with its own image and hadn't noticed that guests were sneaking off to have more fun somewhere else while it wasn't looking. We were working in a very conservative industry that only changed if you forced it and, as Sébastien Bazin said: 'Airbnb has forced us to rethink who we are.'

The sector was truly ripe for change, with identikit brands offering the finest in time warps and inconvenience, a stay in a hotel becoming synonymous with hassle, lost bags and lackadaisical service. For Frits van Paasschen: 'Disruption happens when something doesn't make sense. Waiting in line to show your credit card at a hotel doesn't make sense if you've stayed there a dozen times before and you can pay for an Uber with a couple of taps of a finger on your cell phone. Not really being able to understand what is a great thing to do in a city because you've got thousands of reviews by people who aren't at all like you means that there's a better way for us to understand what we're getting into. There are a thousand lines and hassle and inconveniences. Travel is inconvenient. It's anonymous because it's not personalised. It's uncertain because you don't know what you're getting into. Those are all things that don't make sense in a world where the flow of information is smooth, limitless and free.'

More disruption would come, as more people travelled and more of them found themselves staring into space in the line to have their passports checked or wondering why they were hungry at 3am and there was nothing to eat. But that disruption was unlikely to come from Airbnb, which had found its place, providing a segment of stay that had been lacking and a way to get it quickly and easily to consumers. The signs suggested that it would get deeper into the OTA space, becoming a supplier of its specialised inventory and the means to reach it, too. Airbnb was a piece of technology, an investor tool, an aggregator of supply.

The company had, after all, never claimed to be a hospitality company. In its most-recent funding round, the SEC filing[1] listed itself as 'other technology travel'. There have even been suggestions that it could utilise its vast crates of consumer data and make its way deeper into technology. Or maybe it would just buy a hotel company or be bought itself. For Clarice and her loom, the platform would remain a route to a bit of an income on the side, as long as she paid her tax and installed a smoke detector. For those professional investors who wanted to rent out entire floors, the future in crowded metropolises was less certain and, for the platform's 'live there' ethos, this might be no bad thing.

---

[1] www.sec.gov/Archives/edgar/data/1559720/000155972017000001/xslFormDX01/primary_doc.xml

The next wave of disruption was expected from Google, Facebook, the start-up in next-door's garage, all looking at the $8 trillion travel sector and trying to work out how to take a slice. The time of Airbnb keeping hoteliers awake has largely passed and some new monster will take up residence under their beds.

Hotels have responded to the homesharing threat and the sector was, for the first time in many decades, producing hotels that were exciting across the range of hotel guests, not just those who could afford to be wrapped in silk and carried from their Learjets to their gold and gossamer suites. Hotels have realised that they have to cater to other sorts of guests, that not all of them will be sleeping over and that not all of them will fit neatly into their identical boxes. The challenge will be to bring soul to scale, with the drive coming, unexpectedly, from a French CEO with a background in finance who used to run a football club.

It's not over. Amar Lalvani[2], CEO of Standard Hotels, claimed that the trend shift had already come, that the next generation working for him would look at the alternatives to hotels when they were travelling before they considered a hotel. While hotels had been forced to notice the leisure market, with its inconvenient groups and families, what would be the next segment to be disrupted? The OTAs and peer-to-peer lodging captured the imagination and wallet of the leisure traveller, but what would happen when something came along that wanted to go after that corporate traveller, so happy eating their cooling club sandwich alone in their room?

That hotels had started to appreciate the need to change was apparent in the rapid disgorgement of brands. But some will be left behind. The mid-market has become a dead zone, devoid of innovation, pressured on price from below and on service from above. The only reason to

---

[2]So he told the International Hotel Investment Forum in 2019, and it went down about as well as you can imagine.

stay in one of those globe-spanning brands was for the convenience of location and to clock up loyalty points. Even before the arrival of Airbnb, the proliferation of brands had started to eat the mid-market alive and segmentation in the sector was likely to look very different in the future as a result. It will not be missed.

The consumer has become more demanding and will not give up on its demands for exactly what it wants exactly when it wants it. What this looks like can change from one moment to the next, and those brands looking dewy-eyed at millennials for their next room night were likely to find themselves outmoded when outbound Chinese travel got properly underway.

What the sector had started to get a grip on was that not all consumers were the same. What it has remembered is its passion and for that, Imran Hussain, take it away: 'If you're not in this business to put on a show, you're probably in the wrong business and for that reason I could never see something like Airbnb as the competition. The only thing that they have in common with us is they both have a bed with a pillow on it. You have to see how much somebody wants something before you really value it, or see the struggles that they went through before you really understand it. Nobody on the Airbnb team ever sweated, bled, cried and nearly tore their hair out on the edge of bankruptcy to realise a vision.

'Hotels are an opportunity to produce something special and I refuse to believe that is solely regarded as ROIs, projections, forecast and budgets. It's more than that. And what we do is way more than that.'

THANK YOUS

Much and many thanks to all of the below, without whom this book would be just be an extended rant in the Marlene Bar.

Front of House:
Dirk Bakker, CEO, Colliers International, the Netherlands
Sébastien Bazin, chairman and CEO, Accor
James Bland, director, BVA BDRC
Tom Carroll, head of EMEA corporate research, JLL
Jim Cathcart, director of policy and regulation, UKHospitality
James Chappell, global business director, Horwath HTL
Puneet Chhatwal, MD and CEO, Indian Hotels Company
Marieke Dessauvagie, hotel consultant, Colliers International
Thomas Emanuel, director, STR
Mark Essex, director, public policy, KPMG
Cindy Estis Green, CEO and co-founder, Kalibri Labs
David Harper, head of hotel valuations, Hotel Partners Africa
Christoph Hoffmann, CEO, 25hours Hotels
Imran Hussain, director, THC/Endeavour
Jessica Jahns, head of EMEA Hotels & Hospitality research, JLL
Lily McIlwain, head of content, Triptease
Lennert de Jong, commercial director, citizenM
Dexter Moren, founding director, Dexter Moren Associates
Kate Nicholls, CEO, UKHospitality
Charlie Osmond, founder and chief tease, Triptease
Frits van Paasschen, author, citizenM advisory board, former Starwood Hotels & Resorts president and CEO
Guy Parsons, CEO, easyHotel
Tim Ramskill, managing director, head of EMEA equity research, Credit Suisse
Jeremy Robson, owner, Great Northern Hotel
Robin Sheppard, chairman, Bespoke Hotels
Simona Thompson, owner, 4 Percy Place,
John Wagner, director, Cycas Hospitality
John Webber, head of rating, Colliers International
James Woudhuysen, visiting professor, London South Bank University

The back office:
Daniel Braham (*the hotel sector IS like the plot of* The Usual Suspects)
Anya Clifton (*sufferer of the book thesis ad nauseam in Chapter One*)

Alice Doggrell *(aunting above and beyond)*
Danny Fryer and Lara *(shallow and successful)*
Alexi Khajavi *(work hard and be childish)*
Philip Ward *(I blame you)*

The GM:
Ian Hallsworth at Bloomsbury Publishing, with the tireless help of Allie Collins, Kealey Rigden and Matt James

INDEX